Contents

v

Preface

This book is a short introduction to a wide variety of models for the description, analysis, and optimization of some of the main features of present-day cities. It seeks to bridge the gap between generally useful applied mathematics (such as calculus, probability, linear models) and the rapidly growing specialized research literature on techniques for urban analysis. It is aimed specifically at students in systems engineering and operations research, industrial engineering, transportation planning, and civil engineering. It should also be useful to students of urban planning and public administration, provided that they have prerequisite knowledge of college-level calculus.

"Urban system" is a term used rather indiscriminately to describe almost any activity which concerns society. It seems that only farming, fishing, and mineral extraction are excluded, provided that these proceed in remote areas and have no measurable environmental fallout. The present book, far more modest in scope, is concerned mainly with the *tools* for analyzing population, land use, transportation networks, public facility siting, and resource allocation in congested urban environments. With some exceptions, notably in public health and criminal justice, it does not consider areas of public administration that are not necessarily intertwined with the urban structure as a specific and usually crowded place on the map. Even within its scope, the book omits some systems, such as those for sewage disposal, which today are so sophisticated that useful presentation requires very extensive preparatory knowledge.

The material is appropriate for a one-term course at the senior or graduate level. The work can, in principle, be enriched significantly by the assignment of real-world projects whereby the student obtains first-hand experience in problem formulation, data collection, analysis, and presentation of results. But in the author's experience such projects are fully successful only for well-motivated students who are given adequate time and academic credit, substantial faculty guidance, and suitable introductions to pertinent public officials. Because these conditions are hard to meet, the text is organized in a classical manner whereby illustrations and problems are offered as at least a partial substitute for field experience.

It is intended that the book be suitable for students with quite varied backgrounds. To this end, the only specific prerequisite is some knowledge of calculus. However, the subject matter is complicated, the pace is brisk, and several topics require the use of elementary probability and differential equations. Even though much effort has been devoted toward simplifying and explaining the mathematical apparatus, minimally prepared students ought be forewarned that they may have to engage in some collateral study as the course proceeds.

No knowledge is assumed and no material is presented on the use of electronic computers. Yet many of the exhibited models are unwieldy for practical application unless programmed for such machines. Therefore the serious student surely ought to familiarize himself with one or more of the major computer simulation languages.

Because the subject matter of this book is relatively new, the author would be especially grateful for corrections, criticisms, and suggestions for improvement.

Chapter *1*

Introduction

1-1 On the Use of This Book

The book exhibits and explains many models intended to aid the study of urban problems. The models are idealized "paper-and-pencil" representations of real-life processes. The analyst uses them to simulate society's behavior in response to alternative managerial stimuli.

The material herein is in no sense an introduction to the practice of urban planning. Except in occasional illustrations, there is almost no consideration of actual urban history, social and economic life, administrative practices, or technology for transportation, services, and utilities. This self-imposed limitation, to modeling methodology rather than the description of actual society, is unimportant to a reader with substantial knowledge of urban history and present behavior. In the absence of such a background, a student might well engage in a modest program of collateral reading. The literature on the subject is enormous; hence the author offers a short list of books [1–8] which he has found to be particularly instructive and enjoyable.

It is assumed that the reader is familiar with elementary calculus. In addition, some concepts in elementary probability and linear algebra are defined and used with only a very limited amount of introductory discussion. If the reader, therefore, encounters mathematical difficulties, he may find effective help in References [9–13]. The author particularly recommends the succinct and clear text by Hillier and Lieberman [9].

This first chapter offers a short general discussion, followed by illus-

1

trations of a few basic modeling approaches for urban analysis. Subsequent chapters present many further models for simulating, and sometimes optimizing, population change, the economy, land use, transportation, congestion, facility location, and the allocation of resources. Special emphasis is placed on transportation and the general treatment of congestion because these are better understood, or at least have been studied longer, than some other equally important topics.

The models are shown in a general and often simplified way, and it ought to be kept in mind that much remains to be done when one seeks to adapt one of them to describe a particular real process. A model's utility is established only if it can be shown to simulate reality in a reasonably accurate way. Usually this is done by "calibrating" it to reproduce as well as possible observed or observable present or past behavior. One's confidence in the model, then, will be proportional to the degree of accuracy perceived in the reproduction. Calibration will be considered briefly for some of the models. However, it should be pointed out that first-rate calibration often requires sophisticated statistical analysis beyond the scope of this book. Further, even when a model "passes" a calibration test, it may "fail" in use if the future environment is so unfair as to differ significantly from the one assumed for the test. It thus behooves the modeler to maintain some degree of modesty regarding the level of certainty to be expected from his work.

A number of problems are offered at the end of most chapters. These problems often do not have unique correct solutions. Some neither call for nor are susceptible to solution in the sense generally accepted in mathematics or engineering science. Being open ended, they can be answered at quite varied levels of effort and sophistication. It is hoped that they prove to be useful exercises toward understanding and exploiting the material offered here.

No attempt has been made to develop a really comprehensive list of references. If a model or technique is presented without source documentation, it either has been generally well known for a long time or it has been especially designed for the present work.

1-2 What Is an Urban Area?

It is not easy to define an urban area in a way that differentiates it unambiguously from the remainder of the inhabited world. In the past, the usual criteria were population and land use. If an area had a population density of more than about 2500 persons per square mile and if most of the land was used by people for purposes other than agriculture, then the area was viewed as urban.

Today this definition is deficient. Aided by widespread automobile ownership, urban settlements cover increasingly large areas and mingle with long-established agricultural enterprises. Even in many entirely rural regions, the mass of the population is engaged in specialized occupations other than farming. Thus, it has become appropriate to view the urban area as a social rather than a physical entity. A region is urban wherever the population is characterized by great specialization of labor, with consequent interdependence, and the society requires extensive managerial organization to provide services deemed essential for civilized survival.

Despite these changes, the most pressing urban problems still are those caused by congestion. A normal and continuing main concern of an urban population is the use made of its land. This limited resource must be allocated, developed, and managed to meet the needs of housing, industry, recreation, transportation, water supply, and waste disposal. Police and fire protection services also are victims of congestion, the first because proximity among people multiplies opportunities and inducements for crime, the latter because closely spaced residences can ignite one another.

On the other hand, many social services, such as the educational establishment, health delivery systems, and public welfare administrations, are not directly affected by congestion. They are viewed as peculiarly urban concerns in the United States today because

(1) the majority of the population lives in urban areas;

(2) recent mass immigration from impoverished rural enclaves to old city centers has accentuated urban social conflicts;

(3) *local* government is charged with the management of public social services.

In a more centrally managed society, such as that of France, these activities are budgeted and planned nationally and thus are less likely to be viewed as peculiarly urban.

Until the advent of the automobile, large cities were very densely populated to make possible travel by foot or by high-cost, high-density public transit. Population densities in excess of 100,000 persons per square mile were common. Today almost all of those areas, still occupied at such densities, are losing population, and there is a continuing outward spread of residences, at the edges of cities, at population densities dramatically lower than ever before. We are in the midst of the development of a very low population density urban life style, which is totally dependent on the ubiquity of private automobiles.

TABLE 1-1 Urban Areas—Comparative Statistics[a]

	Year	Manhattan	New York City	"Greater New York"[b]	Megalopolis	United States
Physical characteristics:						
Area, in square miles	1970	22.3	316	3939	53,575	3,615,210
Percent used for streets	1960	35.5	30.1	—	—	1
Percent used for farms and pasture	1954	0	0.7	10.5	35	61
Population:						
Total resident in thousands	1970	1539	7868	15,560	41,000	203,166
Change, 1960-70, %	—	-9.4	+1.0	+8.4	+10.2	+13.3
Density, persons per square mile	1970	69,000	24,900	4530	760	56
Employment:						
Total employment in thousands	1970	2205	3838	6422	—	70,600
Management:						
Number of the 500 largest industrial corporations with headquarters in given area, from *Fortune Magazine* survey	1962	133	134	155	208	499
	1973	105	106	149	184	499
Communications and transportation:						
Number of telephones per 1000 residents	1962	1120	550	460	—	375
Number of automobiles per 1000 residents	1971	—	205	—	—	454
Median home-to-work commuting time for those who work in area, minutes	1956	59	—	42	—	—
Proportion of workers in area who commute by						
Car and taxi, %	1951–1960	11	—	41	—	68
Bus, %	1951–1960	5	—	14	—	}15
Railroad and rapid transit	1951–1960	81	—	33	—	
Foot and other, %	1951–1960	3	—	12	—	17

[a] From the literature [3, 28, 29, 33].

[b] "Greater New York" here includes the following standard metropolitan statistical areas: New York, Jersey City, Newark, Paterson, and Stamford, as defined by the United States Census Bureau.

4

At this point, it is appropriate to offer some quantitative information to illustrate features of urban life. It would be misleading to exhibit averages for all cities. The differences in employment, land use, and residence patterns between a Boston and a Los Angeles, between a Chicago and a Paris are much too great for simple generalizations. Consequently, we exhibit in Table 1-1 some facts about a few selected specific areas. The selected group consists of a nested set of five regions. The smallest is the borough of Manhattan in New York City, tremendously congested, with a large residential population and an even greater working population. Next in size is New York City, including Manhattan. New York is a political entity and one of the world's largest cities. However, New York contains only about half the people who inhabit its metropolitan area, often called "Greater New York." Five standard metropolitan statistical areas, delineated by the United States Census Bureau, are combined here for this region—our third example. However, even this area is closely interdependent with other cities that overlap its edges. One may well view the entire northeastern seaboard of the United States, from Boston to Washington, as a single urban entity. Delineated and named "megalopolis" by the geographer Jean Gottmann [3], this area is the fourth illustration. The entire United States is exhibited for a final comparison.

Some of the facts shown in Table 1-1 deserve special comment:

1. The greater the population density, the greater is the proportion of land devoted to transportation.

2. The greater the population density, the slower is the rise of population with time. Population today actually declines with time if its density is too great for universal automobile ownership.

3. Manhattan's high population density and its position as the central business district of the nation's largest city make it unique. Note that more people work there than live there, the low car ownership, and the concentration of corporate headquarters.

1-3 The Modeling of Urban Processes

The ideal way to learn about any process or activity is to observe it at work in its natural environment both with and without a variety of constraining stimuli. Such full-scale field work can be awkward, expensive, and politically unpalatable for many significant urban activities such as town development, commuter travel, and major government services. Hence one seeks to simulate these activities with the aid of models, which can be studied on paper, digital computer, or other "laboratory" facility. If a segment of past behavior by a real system can be thus modeled with some degree of at least qualitative accuracy, then perhaps the model will offer useful insights when it is used to parallel future real behavior under changed conditions.

Because urban systems usually involve large numbers of quite sophisticated elements—i.e., people—the following difficulties are likely to confront the modeler:

(a) It is impossible to model a process in full deterministic detail. Thus, a model is likely to be a probabilistic representation of real life, although it may often be appropriate to suppress explicitly probabilistic mathematics by dealing only with "expected," or average, behavior.

(b) The real world usually is only partially understood. Even where understanding is good, factual information, required for model calibration, is likely to be expensive or difficult to obtain. For example, one understands quite clearly that commuting by car requires access to a car. Yet it may take an enormous survey to deduce the circumstances under which poor persons have access to automotive transport.

Models may be static or dynamic. A static model describes the equilibrium behavior of a system wherein little or nothing changes with time. A dynamic model describes how a system evolves through time, naturally or in response to stimuli.

The simplest possible dynamic models extrapolate simple observed trends. Such extrapolation is insufficient if one is concerned with the effects of stimuli that have not been observed previously. The past growth pattern of an isolated island is no guide to future growth once the island is newly connected to the mainland by a bridge. To cope with this sort of problem, one seeks to design "behavioral" models in which there are some explicit relationships between stimuli and the consequent reactions. Though one may easily go wrong in postulating cause–effect relations for situations not yet observed in real life, this is sometimes necessary to achieve *any* insight into future behavior.

Some activities of interest, such as the uses of leisure time, the timing of fires or other emergencies, and the production of sewage material, ought not or cannot be subject to much direct control for optimal behavior. For these activities, models ought to predict uncontrolled behavior so that there may be suitable and effective plans for government accommodation to the inevitable.

Some other activities, such as violent crimes against persons, traffic conflicts at intersections, and the spread of contagious diseases, (1) are susceptible to control, and (2) call for control objectives that are reasonably self-evident and noncontroversial. For these, models should permit repeated simulation under all reasonable alternative stimuli, so that the effects of differing control mechanisms can be compared. One then "optimizes" by identifying and implementing the course of action that appears most effective on the basis of the agreed objectives.

The vast majority of urban activities fall between these two extremes. They are susceptible to control, but one or more impediments exist:

(a) People may feel, perhaps justly, that such control is partially or wholly an intolerable incursion on private freedom of choice.

(b) Control may be generally acceptable, but it may not be clear what the optimizing criterion ought to be.

(c) Control may be acceptable, with agreed-upon criteria, but the criteria conflict with one another.

For such activities, the analyst ought to use model simulation to provide a number of meaningful alternative activity scenarios as inputs to the society's decision process.

It is far from trivial to deduce what constitutes ideal or optimum system performance in a particular environment. Consider, for example, the control of rush hour commuter travel. One might argue for any of the following inconsistent criteria:

1. The minimization of the average commuter's travel time.

2. The minimization of the day-to-day variance in the average commuter's travel time. For example, it may be thought more desirable to get to work in 40 ± 5 minutes than in 30 ± 20 minutes.

3. The minimization of the travel time variance among all commuters, thus giving priority to those who travel farthest.

4. The minimization of transit travel time, at the expense of the private car, so as to discourage commuting by private car.

5. The minimization of the number of persons who have to commute to outside their home neighborhoods. Here, the traffic control function would be transmogrified into a traffic plan, abetted by appropriate construction zoning, which would encourage commercial decentralization.

Obviously, this list could go on and on. But even if one considers only the above five alternatives, one faces a dilemma which can only be resolved by a political judgment of what is best. Policies that achieve any one of the objectives are likely to be inimical to the others.

1-4 Illustrations

The following examples exhibit very idealized situations in equilibrium. It should be emphasized that real-world applications require the addition and analysis of many further details.

(a) *Smeed's Land-Use Model* .

R. J. Smeed has developed a simple land-use accounting model aimed at deducing the space required by a town center, given the means by which commuters travel. Here follows a simplified version of Smeed's original model [32].

The minimum area required by a central business district consists of the space required for the work performed therein, the space required for commuters to reach their places of work, and the space, if any, required to park their vehicles.

To deduce the ground area required for travel, one must know the flow capacity c, in persons per unit time, of a roadway of width w. If the roadway is used at peak capacity for a rush period time T, the number of persons who can be carried during this period per unit width of roadway is cT/w. The roadway width λ, required by one person, is the inverse of this, namely, $\lambda = w/cT$. The area of roadway required for one peak period journey of length L is

$$A = L(w/cT) = L\lambda. \qquad (1\text{-}1)$$

Table 1-2 gives typical values of λ for various modes of transport on the basis of British experience and on the assumption that the busy period T

TABLE 1-2

Carrying Capacities of Varying Types of Roadway and Associated Areas Required per Person during Peak Period for a One-Mile Journey[a,b]

Mode of transport	Flow (number of persons per foot width per hour)	Speed (mph)	λ (feet)	Area required per person (square feet)
Automobiles on urban street 44 feet wide with 1.5 passengers per vehicle	67	15	0.0074	39
	95	10	0.00526	28
Automobiles on urban expressway with 1.5 passengers/ vehicle	187	40	0.0027	14
Pedestrian way	800	2.5	0.0006	3
Urban railway line	2900	18	0.00017	0.9
	2200	30	0.00023	1.2

[a] Source: Smeed [32].

[b] Daily peak busy period: $T = 2$ hours.

is of two-hours' duration. Also shown are the corresponding values of area required for a one-mile journey.

Suppose that the smallest central business district, sufficient to accommodate N workers, is represented by a circle of radius r. Suppose further that all work places are uniformly distributed throughout this district and that all places of residence are outside, with circular symmetry. Assume that "in his journey to work, the worker travels along a straight line from his residence to the town center until he reaches radius r. He then travels directly toward the place at which he works, the position of which is not correlated with the place at which he lives or with the point at which he reaches the outer boundary of the town center." [32]

Smeed deduces that the average of distances, from one point at radius r to all points within the circle of radius r, is about $1.36r$, given the restrictions imposed on travel by a rectangular street grid. Hence the distance traveled in the central business district by N workers is $1.36Nr$, and the minimum area required for roadway is $1.36Nr\lambda$.

Each worker requires also a ground space G for work and a space P for parking. P is assumed to be zero unless the worker travels by automobile. The sum of the areas, required for roadway, for work, and for parking, is equal to the minimum area of the central business district. Hence

$$1.36Nr\lambda + N(G + P) = \pi r^2,$$

with solution

$$r = 0.216N\lambda \left[\left(1 + \frac{G + P}{0.147N\lambda^2} \right)^{1/2} + 1 \right]. \tag{1-2}$$

To examine the general behavior of this equation, Smeed set $G = 100$ square feet as the net ground space required per person for work, $P = 133$ square feet per person for ground-level parking, and $P = 13.3$ square feet per person for multilevel parking. The figures are hypothetical and are based on British office building space requirements, car sizes, and on 1.5 commuters per car. The multilevel parking space is based on garages with at least 10 levels and so represents a practical minimum.

Table 1-3 lists some of the results obtained by substituting these figures and the appropriate values of λ into Eq. (1-2). It is evident that, first, roadway space increases much more rapidly than the number of workers, and, second, that if everyone travels by car, large town centers require more space for roadway than for parking even if all parking is at ground level. The second conclusion is most remarkable. In judging these figures, one should recall that present-day central business districts devote from 15% (Tokyo) to 35% (New York) to 70% (Los Angeles) of their land to streets and sidewalks.

TABLE 1-3
Radius r of Central Business District and % of Ground Area Devoted to
(a) Roadway, (b) Parking, and (c) Working Space[a]

Mode of travel to center	Nature of parking	Area (P) for parking per person (square feet)	Working population in town center		
			50,000	500,000	5,000,000
			r† (a, b, c)‡	r† (a, b, c)‡	r† (a, b, c)‡
Urban railway $\lambda = 0.00023$	—	0	0.24 (0.3, 0, 99.7)	0.76 (1, 0, 99)	2.44 (4, 0, 96)
Car on expressway $\lambda = 0.0027$	Multi-level	13.3	0.26 (4, 11, 85)	0.86 (13, 10, 77)	3.16 (34, 8, 58)
Car on expressway $\lambda = 0.0027$	Ground level	133	0.37 (3, 55, 42)	1.21 (9, 52, 39)	4.24 (25, 42, 23)
Car on 44 ft street $\lambda = 0.0074$	Multi-level	13.3	0.27 (11, 10, 79)	0.97 (31, 8, 71)	4.48 (67, 4, 29)
Car on 44 ft street $\lambda = 0.0074$	Ground level	133	0.38 (8, 53, 39)	1.32 (23, 44, 33)	5.47 (55, 25, 20)

[a] *Source*: Smeed [32].
† Radius r miles.
‡ Percentage of ground area.

Models of this type can be used to study the effects of circumferential roadways, open space in the middle of the city, and more complex problems. They have been developed further for central business districts by Lam and Newell [30] and for satellite town commuting by Tan [34].

(b) Manpower Scheduling

Suppose a town police department faces the minimum manpower requirements during each successive day (Table 1-4). Suppose further that

TABLE 1-4

Period	Time of day (24-hr-clock)	Minimum number of policemen
1	0–4	3
2	4–8	2
3	8–12	4
4	12–16	5
5	16–20	6
6	20–24	8

policemen work only simple 8-hour shifts. It is required to find a manpower schedule that minimizes the number of policemen used.

Let

$$x_{12} = \text{number of policemen assigned to periods 1–2}$$

$$x_{23} = \text{number of policemen assigned to periods 2–3}$$

$$x_{34} = \text{number of policemen assigned to periods 3–4}$$

$$x_{45} = \text{number of policemen assigned to periods 4–5}$$

$$x_{56} = \text{number of policemen assigned to periods 5–6}$$

$$x_{61} = \text{number of policemen assigned to periods 6–1}$$

The total number of policemen assigned to a 24-hour day is

$$F = x_{12} + x_{23} + x_{34} + x_{45} + x_{56} + x_{61}.$$

The problem is to minimize F, subject to the given manpower requirements:

$$x_{12} + x_{23} \geq 2, \quad x_{23} + x_{34} \geq 4,$$

$$x_{34} + x_{45} \geq 5, \quad x_{45} + x_{56} \geq 6,$$

$$x_{56} + x_{61} \geq 8, \quad x_{61} + x_{12} \geq 3.$$

To ensure realism, it is also necessary to specify that all the x_{ij}'s be integers greater than or equal to zero.

Once formulated in this manner, the policeman scheduling problem is called an "integer linear program." The formal methodology for minimizing F is described in texts on linear programming and will not be considered here. However, it may be of interest to note that the particular example here has several optimal solutions, all of which require 15 men in order to cover the 14-man shifts implied by the requirements table. One solution is $x_{12} = 0$, $x_{23} = 2$, $x_{34} = 2$, $x_{45} = 3$, $x_{56} = 5$, and $x_{61} = 3$.

Further discussion on manpower scheduling can be found in Reference [10].

(c) *Demand for Maternity Hospital Facilities*

The problem is to decide how many maternity beds should be provided in a community hospital. Suppose that the hospital is to serve 4000 women of childbearing age, that these 4000 women are expected to have a total of 400 babies per year, and that the average hospital stay is 5 days.

Since the actual number of mothers at the hospital on any one day cannot be known exactly, the problem must be handled probabilistically. A reasonable way to do this is to adopt an appropriate "level of service" standard. The one chosen here is:

"On the average, it is acceptable to have insufficient beds on not more than K days per year."

The first step is to construct a model that will predict the probability P_n (overflow) that more than n beds are required on any one day. Then the level of service criterion will be implemented most cheaply if one provides the smallest number of beds, which yields

$$P_n \text{ (overflow)} \leq K/365.$$

The following assumptions are made to simplify the model:

1.   The expected number of births per day does not vary either with the day of the week or the week of the year.
2.   All fertile women are equally likely to have babies on any one day.
3.   Multiple births—twins, triplets, etc.—need not be considered.
4.   Each woman spends exactly five days in the hospital.

A thorough analysis ought include investigation of how sensitive the results are to these assumptions.

By assumption 4, the number of mothers in the hospital, on any one day, is equal to the number who entered the hospital in the five-day period ending on that day. By assumptions 1–3, this number is predicted by the probability distribution for the number of births in *any* five-day period. Let P be the probability that any fertile woman gives birth to a baby during any five-day period. Then the probability $B_n(N, P)$, that n babies are born to N women in any five-day period, is given by the binomial distribution:

$$B_n(N, P) = \binom{N}{n} P^n (1 - P)^{N-n}, \quad \text{where} \quad \binom{N}{n} = \frac{N!}{n!(N - n)!}.$$

The above equation is awkward to use for large values of N. However, with N large and P small, a good approximation is given by the Poisson distribution $P_n(NP)$, for which

$$B_n(N, P) \cong P_n(NP) = \frac{(NP)^n e^{-NP}}{n!}.$$

If the reader is not reasonably familiar with these distributions, he ought to review some probability theory. Chapter 3 of the book by Hillier and Lieberman [9] may be most useful to this end.

The selected level of service measure is

P_n (overflow) $= 1 -$ probability of n or fewer births in 5 days

$$= 1 - \sum_{i=0}^{n} B_n(N, P) \cong 1 - \sum_{i=0}^{n} P_n(NP).$$

Since the expected number of births per year is 400, the expected number NP of births in a five-day period is $400(5/365) = 5.5$. By direct calculation, or by reference to a table of the Poisson distribution, one obtains the values given in Table 1-5. If one is prepared to accept overflow on $K = 1$ day per year, then P_n (overflow) should be less than $(1/365 = 0.0027$. The table shows that $n = 13$, for which P_n (overflow) $= 0.001656$, is the smallest number of beds that will provide the given level of service.

TABLE 1-5

n	$P_n(5.5)$	P_n (overflow)
0	0.004087	0.995913
1	0.022478	0.973435
2	0.061816	0.911619
3	0.113327	0.798292
4	0.155825	0.642467
5	0.171407	0.471059
6	0.157124	0.313936
7	0.123451	0.190485
8	0.084872	0.105613
9	0.051867	0.053747
10	0.028526	0.025221
11	0.014263	0.010958
12	0.006536	0.004422
13	0.002766	0.001656
14	0.001086	0.000570

(d) *Individual versus Collective Optimization*

A basic function of government is the regulation of individual behavior so as to obtain maximum benefits for society as a whole. Based on this premise, it would seem appropriate for government to engage in regulation if and only if such regulation does result in greater overall benefits than would accrue without it. The example below shows that application of this principle is not entirely obvious and that there easily can be conflict between fair treatment for individuals and maximum good for the society as a whole.

Suppose that 1200 cars travel each hour from point A to point B. Let there be two roads between A and B. One road is direct and faster than the other. However, both roads are subject to congestion, and traffic is slowed down when they are crowded. The expected travel times from A to B are given in Table 1-6. If drivers are left alone to choose their own

TABLE 1-6

Flow in cars per hour	Expected travel time in hours	
	Fast road	Slow road
fewer than 1000	0.50	0.80
1100	0.55	0.85
1200	0.60	0.90
1300	0.70	1.00
1400	0.80	1.15
1500	1.00	1.35

routes, almost all of them will choose the faster road. Therefore, the slow road would get significant traffic only when the overall flow from A to B exceeds 1400 cars per hour. At the given flow figure of 1200 cars per hour, practically everyone goes on the fast road. The total time invested in travel during each hour is

$$(1200 \text{ cars per hour})(0.60 \text{ hours}) = 720 \text{ hours}.$$

It might be possible for society to coerce some of the cars to take the slow road. If 200 cars per hour were thus diverted, the total travel time investment per hour would drop to

$$(1000 \text{ cars per hour})(0.50 \text{ hours}) + (200 \text{ cars per hour})(0.80 \text{ hours})$$

$$= 660 \text{ hours}.$$

There would be a saving of 60 hours, to society as a whole, during every hour that the roads are thus used. This would be at the expense of 200 drivers each hour, each of whom would spend 0.20 hour more than before.

Unfortunately, there is no pat answer to the question of whether a minority should be penalized for the good of society as a whole. The best the analyst can do is to clearly evaluate the alternatives.

This illustration is adapted from a well-known observation by the economist Pigou [31]. Pigou was concerned with the question of whether and how society should regulate business competition.

PROBLEMS

1. For the neighborhood in which you live, estimate the proportions of land devoted to streets and other transportation facilities, residences, commerce and industry, public recreation, and other purposes. Write a short critique of this allocation wherein you consider how well it works for society.

2. Does your home town have a plan for organizing or controlling growth? If so, what are its main features? Would it be possible for the population to double in 10 years? How would the amenities of local life be affected in the event of such explosive growth?

3. As time passes, there is a general trend to provide more services to the entire population on a tax-supported basis, thus enabling the individual to participate regardless of the level of his own resources. For example, the world is gradually moving toward tax-supported medical services and old age income maintenance. Below are listed some other services that might be offered "free" to every member of society. For each, consider

    (i)   the present subsidy, if any, for low-income consumers;
    (ii) how much the overall scale of the service would expand;
    (iii) how society might change as a result of the "free" offering:

    (a) local public transit,
    (b) long-distance moving expenses for persons changing employment,
    (c) local telephone service,
    (d) residential electric power, and
    (e) child care centers for working mothers.

4. The Manhattan central business district of New York City has an area of about 8 square miles, of which about 35% is devoted to streets and sidewalks. Suppose that a program of 100% off-street parking and of strategic direction reversals for one-way streets is imposed. The effect is estimated to make available 75% of the street–sidewalk space for the useful movement of commuter automobiles. Use Smeed's model to make a "ball-park" estimate of the maximum number of commuters that could reach their jobs by private cars during the 90-minute morning rush period. (Author's estimate: 720,000 persons, with 1.5 persons per car and an average speed of 10 mph.)

6. Consider the police scheduling illustration, Section 1.4(b), with the modification that now policemen may be assigned to either (a) straight 8-hour shifts or (b) split shifts, the latter consisting of two 4-hour work periods separated by a 4-hour nonwork period.

    (a) Reformulate the problem to find the minimum number of men that satisfy the given 24-hour schedule.
    (b) Reformulate the problem to find the number of men required to minimize the *cost* of the 24-hour schedule, given that a policeman is paid 25% more for a split shift than for a straight 8-hour shift.

    It is sufficient to set up the problem; you need not find numerical solutions unless you wish to do so.

REFERENCES

(a) *Classics of Urban Analysis*

[1] Rasmussen, S. E., *London: The Unique City*. Macmillan, New York, 1937. Reprinted by MIT Press, Cambridge, Massachusetts, 1967.

This is *the* classic description and analysis of the growth and consequent character of a great world city. London is seen to be the prototype of the "scattered" city, common today in the automotive age, and it is a vivid contrast to the classic "concentrated" cities of continental Europe, such as Paris and Vienna.

[2] Hall, P., *The World Cities*. McGraw-Hill, New York, 1966.

London, Paris, "Randstad Holland," "Rhine–Ruhr," Moscow, New York, and Tokyo are exhibited, with many fine maps, to show their growth and problems. Particularly interesting are demonstrations that certain rather spread groups of cities, such as the "Rhine–Ruhr" complex, are today merging into single functional entities.

[3] Gottmann, J., *Megalopolis: The Urbanized Northeastern Seaboard of the United States*. 20th Century Fund, New York, 1961. Reprinted by MIT Press, Cambridge, Massachusetts, 1964.

The most intensely urbanized area in the world, analyzed in great depth by a distinguished French geographer.

[4] Mumford, L., *The City in History*. Harcourt, New York, 1961.

A primarily cultural analysis, this book is the culminating achievement of a most brilliant urban critic. The annotated bibliography is superb.

[5] Buchanan, C., ed., *Traffic in Towns*. HM Stationery Office, London, 1963. An abridged version is offered by Penguin Books, London, 1964.

A thorough analysis, with specific examples, of how ill-adapted older cities may perhaps survive the onslaught of the automotive age.

[6] Howard, E., *Tomorrow: A Peaceful Path to Land Reform*. London, 1902. Retitled *Garden Cities of Tomorrow*, it has been reprinted several times, e.g., by the MIT Press, Cambridge, Massachusetts, 1967.

A seminal work on the planning of a new town. Here are admirable strictures on the provision of open space, the separation of pedestrians from vehicular traffic, and the reasons for limiting growth.

[7] Le Corbusier (Pseudonym of C. E. Jeanneret), *Urbanisme*. Paris, 1924. Translated as *The City of Tomorrow and Its Planning*. Harcourt, New York, 1929. Reprinted in *Complete Works of Le Corbusier, Vol 1: 1910–1929*. Museum Books, New York, n.d.

The most influential treatise on planning the skyscraper metropolis. The city is viewed as a machine which should be prepared, in advance, to cater to every requirement of its inhabitants.

[8] Doxiadis, C. A., *Urban Renewal and the Future of the American City*. Public Administration Service, Chicago, Illinois, 1966.

The author is the influential founder of "ekistics," the science of human settlements. He is the head of a most successful, though controversial, planning practice with projects throughout the world. The present book emphasizes spatial strategies.

(b) Mathematical Tools

[9]   Hillier, F. S., and G. J. Lieberman, *Introduction to Operations Research*. Holden-Day, San Francisco, California, 1967.
[10] Wagner, H. M., *Principles of Operations Research with Applications to Managerial Decisions*. Prentice-Hall, Englewood Cliffs, New Jersey, 1969.

These two references introduce probability theory, linear programming and network analysis, dynamic programming, queueing theory, stochastic simulation, and several other mathematical modeling techniques useful for urban analysis.

[11] Feller, W., *An Introduction to Probability Theory and Its Applications*, 2nd ed. Vol. 1. Wiley, New York, 1957.
[12] Parzen, E., *Modern Probability Theory and Its Applications*. Wiley, New York, 1960.

Both of these texts are excellent. They do assume that the reader has a modest knowledge of elementary calculus.

[13] Rogers, A., *Matrix Methods in Urban and Regional Analysis.* Holden-Day, San Francisco, California, 1971.

Though there are many other excellent introductions to matrix algebra, this one may be the best choice because of the aptness of its viewpoint and illustrations.

(c) Journals

The following journals have been important primary sources for new work on urban modeling techniques and applications. The list is not exhaustive.

[14] *American Journal of Sociology*
[15] *American Sociological Review*
[16] *Demography*
[17] *Geographical Review*
[18] *Highway Research Record*
[19] *Journal of Regional Science*
[20] *Journal of the American Institute of Planners*
[21] *Journal of Urban Analysis*
[22] *Management Science*
[23] *Operations Research*
[24] *Socio-Economic Planning Sciences*
[25] *Transportation Research*
[26] *Transportation Science*
[27] *Urban Affairs Quarterly*

(d) Text Documentation

[28] *County and City Data Book.* U. S. Bur. of the Census, Washington, D.C., 1967.
[29] Hub-bound travel in the bi-state metropolitan area, *Bulletin No. 91.* Regional Plan Association, New York, 1959.
[30] Lam, T., and Newell, G., Flow-dependent traffic assignment in a circular city. *Transportation Science* **1,** No. 4, 318–361 (1967).
[31] Pigou, A. C., *The Economics of Welfare,* 4th ed., pp. 810–811. Macmillan, New York, 1938.
[32] Smeed, R. J., *The Traffic Problem in Towns.* Manchester Statist. Soc., England, 1961.
[33] *Statistical Abstract of the United States,* 93rd ed. U.S. Bur. of the Census, Washington, D.C., 1973.
[34] Tan, T., Mathematical model for commuter traffic in satellite towns. *Transportation Science* **1,** No. 1, 6–23 (1967).

Chapter *2*

Population

There are two reasons for starting this book with the consideration of population growth models. First, the forecasting of population, for society as a whole or for a specified group within it, is basic to almost every study on the provision of adequate and efficient public services. Second, even the most elementary population modeling formalism illustrates the advantage of explicit cause–effect analysis as compared to simple extrapolation.

The second reason deserves discussion. Suppose that a population doubled from 1000 to 2000 persons between 1950 and 1970. Simple linear extrapolation would yield an estimate of 3000 persons for 1990. But we all know that such an extrapolation is likely to be very inaccurate. At any moment in time, the rate of population increase, being the difference between the overall birth and death rates, is more likely to be proportional to the population size than it is likely to be constant. This observation on cause and effect in population growth ought to be and can be incorporated into the forecasting model. If this is done, the resultant "birth and death model" no longer is linear and, in the absence of constraints, it will predict an exponential growth rate.

The next section exhibits a basic birth and death formalism to account for a population as time progresses. The following sections show how the model can be applied when resources are limited or where it is necessary to distinguish between two or more groups within the society. Finally, there is a brief description of a comprehensive urban growth model, proposed by J. Forrester, which uses the birth and death approach in a most stimulating and controversial manner.

2-1 The Basic Birth and Death Process

The object is to devise an equation to predict the population $n(t)$ of a group as a function of time t. Since the actual values of $n(t)$ cannot be predicted with certainty because births, deaths, and individual migrations occur at effectively random moments, the model seeks to predict the expected value $E[\bar{n}(t)] = \bar{n}(t)$. The standard definition of expected value is used, namely,

$$E[n(t)] = \bar{n}(t) = \sum_{n=0}^{\infty} nP_n(t),$$

where $P_n(t)$ is the probability that the population consists of precisely n persons at time t.

First, a very simple and intuitive argument will be made for formulating the rate $d\bar{n}(t)/dt$ at which the expected population size changes with time. This will be followed by a more thorough mathematical analysis. The latter clearly exhibits the assumptions made and thus exposes some inherent limitations.

Let $\lambda(t)$ be the average "birthrate" per person at time t, including both new babies and new immigrants into the group. The group's total expected birthrate is the average per-capita rate $\lambda(t)$ multiplied by the expected population $\bar{n}(t)$. To avoid confusion, $\lambda(t)$ will be called the expected "specific birthrate," while the total $\lambda(t)\bar{n}(t)$ will be called the expected "gross birthrate." In the literature, $\lambda(t)$ often is given in terms of births per thousand persons per year. Thus $\lambda(t = 1/1/73) = 0.025$ would be expressed as a rate of 40 births per 1000 persons per year prevailing on January 1, 1973. Similarly, let $\mu(t)$ be the average "death rate" per person at time t, including both natural deaths and emigration. $\mu(t)$ will be called the "specific death rate," and $\mu(t)\bar{n}(t)$ will be called the expected "gross death rate."

At any time t, the expected rate of population increase will be the gross birthrate minus the gross death rate. Thus,

$$\frac{d\bar{n}(t)}{dt} = [\lambda(t) - \mu(t)]\bar{n}(t). \tag{2-1}$$

This first-order differential equation is the basic birth and death model. Specific applications and solutions will be discussed in the following sections. The remainder of this section is devoted to a very fundamental development of Eq. (2-1). While this might be skipped by the reader at a

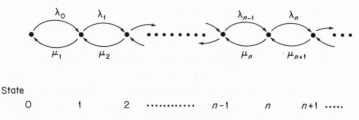

State

0   1   2   ············   *n*-1   *n*   *n*+1 ·····

FIG. 2-1   Transition Diagram for Birth and Death Model

The dots represent possible states of the system or, in the present context, number of persons in the society.

first reading, the material therein is important and will be referred to again later in the book.

One major assumption underlies the probabilistic birth and death equation (2-1). It is that the probability of any one birth or death at any moment in time is assumed to depend only on the population characteristics and external stimuli at that moment. The probability is independent of the actual sequence and timing of all other births or deaths that precede or follow the moment of interest.

Probability models based on the above assumption are called "Markov models" after the mathematician A. A. Markov. Since the assumption forbids any direct relationship between successive births or deaths, the model cannot show explicitly the expected short interval between the births of twins or the correlations among the departure times of an emigrant family. Whether or not there remains sufficient realism is a question that can only be resolved in the context of particular real applications.

Suppose a birth occurs at a moment when there are already precisely n persons in the group. This birth is called a transition from state n to state $n + 1$. Similarly, a death, in an n-person group, is described as a transition from state n to state $n - 1$. For the present model, these two transitions are the only ones that can occur from state n. Figure 2-1 illustrates the model. The points labeled $0, 1, 2, \ldots, n, \ldots$ correspond to $0, 1, 2, \ldots$ persons in the population. The arrows show the allowed transitions.

One must postulate transition probabilities which, hopefully, will provide a reasonable representation of birth and death probabilities in the real population being modeled. Consider an infinitesimally small time interval dt, which begins at time t. Let

$\Pr[(*) \text{ in } dt, \text{ given } n] =$ the probability that whatever is written in place of $(*)$ occurs in the time interval dt, between t and $t + dt$, given that the population size is n at time t.

$\lambda_n(t)$ = a numerical value, ≥ 0, which may depend on population size n and time in history t. Presently, it will be seen that $\lambda_n(t)$ is the same expected gross birthrate defined previously.

$\mu_n(t)$ = a numerical value, ≥ 0, which may depend on population size n and time in history t. It will be used as the expected gross death rate.

We now postulate, quite arbitrarily:

$$\lim_{dt \to 0} \Pr(\text{exactly one birth in } dt, \text{ given } n) = \lambda_n(t) \; dt; \qquad (2\text{-}2a)$$

$$\lim_{dt \to 0} \Pr(\text{exactly one death in } dt, \text{ given } n) = \mu_n(t) \; dt. \qquad (2\text{-}2b)$$

Equation (2-2a) states that the probability of a birth, during an infinitesimally small dt, is proportional to the birthrate $\lambda_n(t)$ and to the time interval dt. In keeping with the Markovian assumption, the probability does not depend on the sequence or times of prior births or deaths. Equation (2-2b) expresses the death probability in the same manner. We further postulate:

$$\lim_{dt \to 0} \Pr \left(\begin{array}{l} \text{two or more events in } dt \text{ where} \\ \text{an event is either a birth or a} \\ \text{death, given } n \end{array} \right) = O(dt^2). \qquad (2\text{-}2c)$$

The expression $O(dt^2)$ is used to describe any quantity that approaches zero at least as fast as dt^2 when $dt \to 0$. Thus, Eq. (2-2c) states that, in an infinitesimal dt, the probability of two or more events is vanishingly small compared to the probability of only one event during the same dt.

It is obvious that in any interval dt there are births and/or deaths or there are not any. Hence

$$\Pr(\text{no births or deaths in } dt, \text{ given } n)$$

$$= 1 - \Pr(\text{one birth in } dt, \text{ given } n)$$

$$- \Pr(\text{one death in } dt, \text{ given } n)$$

$$- \Pr(\text{two or more events in } dt, \text{ given } n)$$

$$= 1 - \lambda_n(t) \; dt - \mu_n(t) \; dt - O(dt^2). \qquad (2\text{-}2d)$$

It is possible to derive a set of probability equations for the population in terms of the postulated transition probabilities. Let

$$P_n(t) = \text{probability that the population size is } n \text{ at time } t.$$

The probability of a population size n, at time $t + dt$, is expressed in terms of the population probabilities at time t and of the transition probabilities for the interval dt between t and $t + dt$:

$$\lim_{dt \to 0} P_n(t + dt) = \Pr(\text{one birth in } dt, \text{ given } n - 1) \cdot P_{n-1}(t)$$

$$+ \Pr(\text{one death in } dt, \text{ given } n + 1) \cdot P_{n+1}(t)$$

$$+ \Pr(\text{no births or deaths in } dt, \text{ given } n) \cdot P_n(t)$$

$$+ O(dt^2)$$

$$= \lambda_{n-1}(t) \, dt \, P_{n-1}(t) + \mu_{n+1}(t) \, dt \, P_{n+1}(t)$$

$$+ [1 - \lambda_n(t) \, dt - \mu_n(t) \, dt - O(dt^2)] P_n(t)$$

$$+ O(dt^2);$$

so

$$\lim_{dt \to 0} \left[\frac{P_n(t + dt) - P_n(t)}{dt} \right] = \lambda_{n-1}(t) P_{n-1}(t) + \mu_{n+1}(t) P_{n+1}(t)$$

$$- [\lambda_n(t) + \mu_n(t)] P_n(t)$$

$$+ \left[\frac{P_n(t) + 1}{dt} \right] O(dt^2).$$

As $dt \to 0$, the left-hand side of this equation becomes the derivative of $P_n(t)$ with respect to time. The last term on the right-hand side approaches zero. Hence

$$\frac{dP_n(t)}{dt} = \lambda_{n-1}(t) P_{n-1}(t) + \mu_{n+1}(t) P_{n+1}(t) - [\lambda_n(t) + \mu_n(t)] P_n(t). \quad (2\text{-}3)$$

Equation (2-3) is the birth and death specialization of an immensely useful equation named for the mathematicians Chapman and Kolmogorov. This equation will appear again in a different guise, Chapter 6, where it will describe the behavior of customers queueing for service.

The gross birthrate $\lambda_n(t)$ usually is proportional to the population size n. Hence it is natural to define a specific birthrate per person $\lambda(t)$; so $\lambda_n(t) = n\lambda(t)$. Similarly, a specific per-capita death rate $\mu(t)$ is defined by $\mu_n(t) = n\mu(t)$. With these substitutions, Eq. (2-3) becomes

$$\frac{dP_n(t)}{dt} = \lambda(t) (n - 1) P_{n-1}(t) + \mu(t) (n + 1) P_{n+1}(t)$$

$$- [\lambda(t) + \mu(t)] n P_n(t). \quad (2\text{-}4)$$

Equation (2-4) actually represents an infinite number of equations for $n = 0, 1, 2, \ldots$, difficult to solve and not directly useful even when a solution is at hand. Such a solution would provide the probabilities $P_n(t)$ for all n, while one really is interested only in the expected population as a function of time. Luckily it is possible to boil down Eq. (2-4) into a single equation in terms of the expected value $E[n(t)]$ of the population. Let $\bar{n}(t) = E[n(t)]$. By definition, this expected value is

$$\bar{n}(t) = E[n(t)] = \sum_{n=0}^{\infty} nP_n(t).$$

Multiply each of the equations (2-4) by n, and then add together all the equations for $n = 0, 1, 2, \ldots$ to get

$$\sum_{n=0}^{\infty} n \frac{dP_n(t)}{dt} = \lambda(t) \sum_{n=0}^{\infty} n(n-1)P_{n-1}(t) + \mu(t) \sum_{n=0}^{\infty} n(n+1)P_{n+1}(t)$$

$$- [\lambda(t) + \mu(t)] \sum_{n=0}^{\infty} n^2 P_n(t). \tag{2-5}$$

Now note that

(a) $\displaystyle \sum_{n=0}^{\infty} n \frac{dP_n(t)}{dt} = \frac{d}{dt} \sum_{n=0}^{\infty} nP_n(t) = \frac{d\bar{n}(t)}{dt}.$

(b)   One cannot have a negative population; so $P_n(t) = 0$ for $n < 0$. Therefore,

$$\sum_{n=0}^{\infty} n(n-1)P_{n-1}(t) = \sum_{n=-1}^{\infty} (n+1)nP_n(t) = \sum_{n=0}^{\infty} (n+1)nP_n(t)$$

$$= \sum_{n=0}^{\infty} n^2 P_n(t) + \sum_{n=0}^{\infty} nP_n(t)$$

$$= \sum_{n=0}^{\infty} n^2 P_n(t) + \bar{n}(t).$$

(c)   Similarly,

$$\sum_{n=0}^{\infty} n(n+1)P_{n+1}(t) = \sum_{n=0}^{\infty} n^2 P_n(t) - \bar{n}(t).$$

Substitute (a), (b), and (c) into Eq. (2-5):

$$\frac{d\bar{n}(t)}{dt} = \lambda(t) \sum_{n=0}^{\infty} n^2 P_n(t) + \lambda(t)\bar{n}(t) + \mu(t) \sum_{n=0}^{\infty} n^2 P_n(t)$$

$$- \mu(t)\bar{n}(t) - [\lambda(t) + \mu(t)] \sum_{n=0}^{\infty} n^2 P_n(t).$$

Finally,

$$\frac{d\bar{n}(t)}{dt} = [\lambda(t) - \mu(t)]\bar{n}(t). \tag{2-6}$$

Equation (2-6) is the same as Eq. (2-1). Thus, the intuitively correct (2-1) is seen to apply when births and deaths are random in the sense defined by the transition probabilities of Eq. (2-2).

2-2   A Closed Society with Unlimited Resources

Suppose there is an isolated society, without immigration or emigration, whose specific birth- and death-rates do not vary with time. In this case, $\lambda(t) = \lambda$, $\mu(t) = \mu$, and Eq. (2-1) becomes

$$\frac{d\bar{n}(t)}{dt} = (\lambda - \mu)\bar{n}(t). \tag{2-7}$$

The solution, checkable by direct substitution in Eq. (2-7), is

$$\bar{n}(t) = \bar{n}(0)e^{(\lambda-\mu)t}, \tag{2-8}$$

where $\bar{n}(0)$ is the population at time $t = 0$. If $(\lambda - \mu) < 0$, the population does not sustain itself and so, as $t \to \infty$, $\bar{n}(t) \to 0$. On the other hand, if $(\lambda - \mu) > 0$, the population increases exponentially with time, and thus grows without any limit. This sort of growth has been observed to occur for limited time periods, but naturally it cannot go on forever. Ultimately the population would outstrip its resources in food or space. Then the death rate would rise because of food shortage or, if the society were capable of planning, the birthrate would decline so as to maintain a viable population.

This simplified population model was first used as a planning tool by Malthus who, in 1798, deduced a most calamitous future for human society.

TABLE 2-1
United States Population Forecast, 1920–2000[a,b]

| | The facts | | | | | The forecast | |
Year	Natural birth-rate (λ_b)	Net migration rate[c] (λ_m)	Natural death rate (μ)	Net rate of increase $(\lambda_b + \lambda_m - \mu)$	Popula-tion	Year	Popula-tion
					$(\times 10^8)$		$(\times 10^8)$
1920	0.0237	+0.0025	0.0130	0.0132	1.065	0	1.065
1925	0.0213	+0.0036	0.0117	0.0132	1.158	5	1.183
1930	0.0189	+0.0019	0.0113	0.0105	1.231	10	1.217
1935	0.0169	−0.0004	0.0109	0.0056	1.273	15	1.300
1940	0.0179	+0.0002	0.0108	0.0073	1.326	20	1.388
1945	0.0195	+0.0004	0.0106	0.0093	1.405	25	1.481
1950	0.0236	+0.0012	0.0096	0.0152	1.523	30	1.582
1955	0.0246	+0.0011	0.0093	0.0164	1.659	35	1.690
1960	0.0237	+0.0022	0.0095	0.0164	1.807	40	1.805
1965	0.0194	+0.0023	0.0094	0.0123	1.935	45	1.928
1970	0.0180	+0.0025	0.0097	0.0108	2.037	50	2.059
1980						60	2.350
1990						70	2.672
2000						80	3.062

[a] Source of Facts: *Statistical Abstract of the United States* [7].
[b] Births, migration, and deaths are given as specific rates in terms of numbers per person per year.
[c] The net migration rates are approximate and are based on five-year averages ending in the years shown.

He felt that birthrates would remain high and that resource expansion was limited so that, ultimately, mass starvation would be the actual mechanism for bringing about $(\lambda - \mu) = 0$.

Do real societies behave in the manner predicted by Eq. (2-8)? The answer is a very qualified yes, but only for those groups where ample resources make possible stable birth and death rates and where migration is not a significant factor. In other circumstances, Eq. (2-8) might be a suitable model for a limited time period.

Let us apply the model to the population of the United States after 1920, subsequent to which time immigration was kept small by statutory barriers. Table 2-1 shows the pertinent facts. The forecaster of 1920 might have tried to use the idealized model (2-8) to predict population for 1970 and subsequently on the basis of 1920 data. If he included the net specific migration rate λ_m, in addition to the natural specific birthrate λ_b, he would

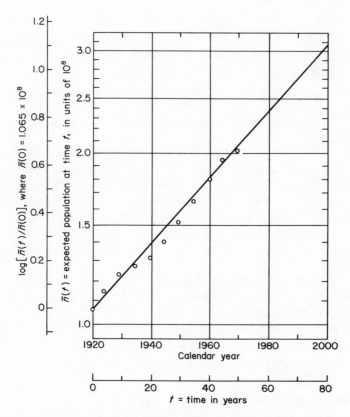

FIG. 2-2   United States Population Forecast, 1920–2000

⊙ = actual population.

have calibrated his model as follows:

$$\bar{n}(0) = 106{,}500{,}000 = 1.065 \times 10^8,$$

where $t = 0$ at some specific moment in 1920.

$\lambda_b = 0.0237,$ the natural specific birthrate in 1920.

$\lambda_m = 0.0025,$ the specific net immigration rate in 1920.

$\mu = 0.0130,$ the natural specific death rate in 1920.

So, from Eq. (2-8):

$$\bar{n}(t) = 1.065 \cdot 10^8 \cdot \exp[(0.0237 + 0.0025 - 0.0130)t]$$

$$= 1.065 \cdot 10^8 \cdot \exp[+0.132t].$$

This forecast $\bar{n}(t)$ is shown in the last column of Table 2-1. The results can be exhibited in a most effective manner by taking the natural logarithm of $[\bar{n}(t)/\bar{n}(0)]$. This act eliminates the exponential and gives the log–linear relation

$$\log[\bar{n}(t)/\bar{n}(0)] = \log[\bar{n}(t)/(1.065 \cdot 10^8)] = +0.0132t.$$

Figure 2-2 compares this relationship to the actual population growth given in Table 2-1.

The 1920 forecaster's model is not very good because he assumed constant birth, death, and migration rates. These rates varied substantially during the subsequent 50 years, so the total specific rate of increase ($\lambda_b + \lambda_m - \mu$) reached a low of 0.0054 in depression 1935 and a high of 0.0164 in 1960. Because the 1920 rate of 0.0132 is intermediate, the numerical forecasts are pretty good for some selected years. The 1960 forecast is almost precisely correct! But in contrast, the 1945 forecast is too large by nearly 8 million persons.

This sort of situation is typical in urban modeling. Even when a model is successful when tested against past behavior, one ought to be quite cautious in claiming great accuracy for the future. Though the 1920 forecast was great for 1960, there is little cause for supposing that its prediction of 306 million, for the year 2000, will turn out as well.

2-3 Finite Resources

The simplest way to model a finite environment is to deduce an $\bar{n}_{\max}$ to represent the largest population that may be sustained. One would postulate that the population would grow exponentially until $\bar{n}_{\max}$ is reached. Subsequently, it would remain constant at $\bar{n}_{\max}$. This sort of growth might well occur in a small area such as a new suburban subdivision. However, in such a case the primary cause of growth is likely to be migration, which will be considered further in Section 2-5.

It is more realistic to expect that, as $\bar{n}(t) \to \bar{n}_{\max}$, the natural rate of increase would decline gradually as the society tries to adapt to its finite environment. Thus, there is likely to be a reduced birthrate supplemented by increased emigration. A very simple model, exhibiting this behavior, sets birth and death rates to be functions of population size as follows:

$$\lambda(t) - \mu(t) = [1 - \bar{n}(t)/\bar{n}_{\max}](\lambda - \mu). \tag{2-9}$$

Here λ and μ are the hypothetical birth- and death rates for the limit

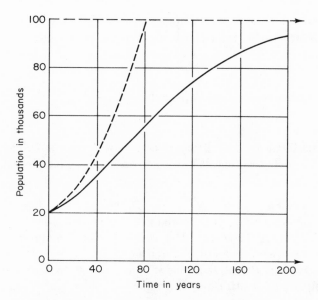

FIG. 2-3   Effect of Limited Resources on Population Growth

——, plot of Eq. (2-10), for constrained growth, with $\bar{n}(0) = 20{,}000$, $\bar{n}_{max} = 100{,}000$, and $(\lambda - \mu) = 0.020$.

– – –, plot of Eq. (2-8), for unconstrained growth, with the same parameters.

$\bar{n}(t) \rightarrow 0$, in which there are no environmental constraints. The multiplier $[1 - \bar{n}(t)/\bar{n}_{max}]$ ensures that growth declines to zero as $\bar{n}(t) \rightarrow n_{max}$. If Eq. (2-9) is substituted into the basic equation (2-1), the solution to the resultant differential equation can be shown to be

$$\bar{n}(t) = \frac{\bar{n}_{max} e^{(\lambda-\mu)t}}{(\bar{n}_{max}/\bar{n}(0)) - 1 + e^{(\lambda-\mu)t}}, \qquad (2\text{-}10)$$

where $\bar{n}(0)$ is the initial population. Equation (2-10) is plotted in Fig. 2-3 for $\bar{n}(0) = 20{,}000$, $\bar{n}_{max} = 100{,}000$, and $(\lambda - \mu) = 0.020$ per person per year. Also shown is a specific growth rate of $(\lambda - \mu) = 0.020$ applied without constraint, Eq. (2-8), until $\bar{n}_{max}$ is reached.

It would be excessively naive to suppose that any real society has quite as simple a resource constraint as has the example here. More realistic constraints, calibrated to fit an actual society, are likely to result in a birth and death equation that cannot be solved analytically. Nevertheless, if these real constraints are clearly understood, they ought to be modeled accurately even though one then faces the need for numerical solution methods. One should remember, however, that it may well be that an idealized formulation, easily manipulated, is just as meaningful as a more pretentious structure if the latter is not fully based in reality.

2-4   The Cohort-Survival Approach

The basic birth and death model embodies a gross simplification. By lumping all people together, it fails to describe important phenomena that result from

(a)   *Imbalances in the Age or Sex Distribution:*   Children are born only to fertile women; death is more likely as one grows older.

(b)   *Economic Differences:*   The rich use more resources, and they may or may not have as many children as do the poor.

(c)   *Social and Racial Differences:*   In addition to significant differences in birth- and death rates, there may be wildly conflicting migration patterns.

To partially overcome these difficulties, the obvious and practical approach is to divide the population into a number of *cohorts*, each consisting of a reasonably homogeneous group of people. One then models the birth and death process separately for each cohort so as to deduce the number who *survive* as time progresses.

The following example illustrates the cohort-survival technique. Let a cohort consist of all the people born during any one year. Let

$\bar{n}_s(t)$ = expected number of persons, born during the year that begins at time s, still alive at time t;

$\lambda_s(t)$ = specific birthrate, at time t, for persons born in the year beginning at time s;

$\mu_s(t)$ = specific death rate, at time t, for persons born in the year beginning at time s.

Consider first the births that occur during the particular year that starts at time r. These births will result in the formation of cohort r with expected cohort population $\bar{n}_r(t)$. At the beginning of the year, the cohort has no members, and so the boundary condition, governing the cohort's birth and death equation, is $\bar{n}_r(t = r) = \bar{n}_r(r) = 0$. As time progresses beyond time r, and until time $r + 1$, all new babies join cohort r. Any cohort s, where $s < r$, might in principle contribute babies during this year. The total birthrate for cohort s at time t is $\lambda_s(t)\bar{n}_s(t)$. The total rate at which babies are born into cohort r, from all preceding cohorts, is

$$\sum_{s=0}^{r-1} \lambda_s(t)\bar{n}_s(t)$$

for all t such that $r \leq t < r + 1$.

The total death rate for cohort r is $\mu_r(t)\bar{n}_r(t)$. Therefore, the first year birth and death equation for cohort r is

$$\frac{d\bar{n}_r(t)}{dt} = \sum_{s=0}^{r-1} \lambda_s(t)\bar{n}_s(t) - \mu_r(t)\bar{n}_r(t) \qquad \text{for} \quad r \leq t < r + 1, \quad \text{(2-11a)}$$

with boundary condition $\bar{n}_r(r) = 0$.

In subsequent years, cohort r can change in size only by the deaths of individuals within it; so

$$\frac{d\bar{n}_r(t)}{dt} = -\mu_r(t)\bar{n}_r(t) \qquad \text{for} \quad t > r + 1. \quad \text{(2-11b)}$$

A cohort-survival analysis almost invariably consists of a number of equations coupled in a rather complex manner. The example, Eqs. (2-11), is particularly simple. Thus, one usually must resort to numerical solution of difference equations, which replace the original system of coupled differential equations. We illustrate with the first-order difference equation equivalent to Eqs. (2-11). Note first that

$$\frac{d\bar{n}_r(t)}{dt} \simeq \frac{\bar{n}_r(t+\tau) - \bar{n}_r(t)}{\tau}$$

if τ is a fairly small increment of time. $\tau = 0.1$ year might be appropriate to population studies. Then

$$\bar{n}_r(t+\tau) = \bar{n}_r(t) + \tau \sum_{s=0}^{r-1} \lambda_s(t)\bar{n}_s(t) - \tau\mu_r(t)\bar{n}_r(t) \qquad \text{(2-12a)}$$

$$\text{for} \quad r \leq t < r + 1,$$

and

$$\bar{n}_r(t+\tau) = \bar{n}_r(t) - \tau\mu_n(t)\bar{n}_s(t) \qquad \text{for} \quad t > r + 1. \quad \text{(2-12b)}$$

Given the values of $\bar{n}_r(t)$ for all $r < t$, the system of equations (2-12) is solved to yield $\bar{n}_r(t+\tau)$. This process is repeated as often as needed. Naturally one ought to use meaningful estimates for the $\lambda_s(t)$ and $\mu_s(t)$.

2-5   Migration

As a cause of population change in a limited area, such as a city or suburb, migration often is of greater importance than is the physical birth and death process. Because migration is the result of complex economic and social stimuli, often obscured by long time lags between causes and effects, there has been little success in the quantitative prediction of local population changes. This has been particularly true when attempts were made to model the movements of particular social or racial cohorts.

In general, the long-term growth and development of an entire urban region, insofar as it differs from society as a whole, are closely related to economic interactions between that region and the greater world about it. While it may be possible to obtain a qualitative picture without detailed economic analysis (see Section 2-6), one really must be prepared to study population change as consequent to and closely linked with industrial development. Chapter 3 will explore the basic methodology for doing this.

The birth and death formalism, without such broad economic analysis, is quite adaptable to the study of short-term population changes due to migration, especially those socially important intraregional displacements, which rapidly change the population composition of established neighborhoods. The following illustration is most tentative and should on no account be taken as an operational model. The idea is to formulate a model that will exhibit a rapid transition from exclusively white to exclusively black occupancy in an old neighborhood of an American city.

Postulate a neighborhood with housing for up to N persons and with no short-term prospect of new construction which might change the value of N. Suppose that, initially at time $t = 0$, the neighborhood is occupied entirely by N whites. These whites have incomes which, on the average, are sufficient to purchase somewhat more luxurious housing than available locally. White persons in other neighborhoods are assumed to be similarly prosperous and thus have no incentive to move into the study area, even if housing were available there.

Let there be a large black population, initially elsewhere in the city. This population, largely ill-housed, is, on the average, able and willing to move into the study area, provided vacant housing is available. It should be noted that, under these circumstances, no blacks can move in until whites move out.

Let $\bar{n}_w(t)$ be the expected number of whites and let $\bar{n}_b(t)$ be the expected number of blacks in the study area at time t. Assume:

(a)   The migration process is so rapid that the natural birth- and death-rates may, in comparison, be ignored.

(b)   The whites have a natural specific emigration rate μ_m, due to actions aimed at securing better housing.

(c)   Some of the whites have a bias against living near blacks. Because of this, there is a bigotry specific emigration rate μ_{mB}, which is proportional to the fraction of the area population that is black. Thus, we postulate

$$\mu_{mB} = c_1 \left[\frac{\bar{n}_b(t)}{\bar{n}_b(t) + \bar{n}_w(t)} \right],$$

where c_1 is a constant.

(d)   The blacks have a natural gross immigration rate, which is proportional to the vacant housing stock $[N - \bar{n}_w(t) - \bar{n}_b(t)]$. Let c_2 be the constant of proportionality.

On the basis of these assumptions, the birth and death equations for the two cohorts are

$$\frac{d\bar{n}_w(t)}{dt} = -[\mu_m + \mu_{mB}]\bar{n}_w(t) = -\left[\mu_m + \frac{c_1 \bar{n}_b(t)}{\bar{n}_b(t) + \bar{n}_w(t)} \right] \bar{n}_w(t),$$

$$\frac{d\bar{n}_b(t)}{dt} = +c_2[N - \bar{n}_w(t) - \bar{n}_b(t)], \qquad (2\text{-}13)$$

with boundary conditions $\bar{n}_w(0) = N$ and $\bar{n}_b(0) = 0$.

As an illustration, suppose that at the beginning of the first year, $t = 0$, an all-white neighborhood consists of $\bar{n}_w(0) = N = 10{,}000$ households. Note that here the household, rather than the individual, will be used as the unit for $\bar{n}_w(t)$, $\bar{n}_b(t)$, and N. Suppose further that conditions (a)–(d) prevail so that the neighborhood is described by Eq. (2-13). Let $\mu_m = 0.03$ and let $c_1 = c_2 = 0.5$.

Figure 2-4 shows what happens in the following 20 years. The model, as expected from its structure, shows a rapid transformation from an all-white to an all-black occupancy. There is a period with many housing vacancies. In the real world the emigrant often stays on, after deciding to leave, until his residence is sold or rented. Thus, the model "vacancies" correspond to real-world housing units for sale or for rent. Emotional descriptions of the high-vacancy period often include pejorative terms such as "block busting" and "panic selling."

It is worth emphasizing that the model behavior depends particularly on the assumption (b) that whites always have a positive net emigration rate regardless of black occupancy. If one wishes to slow the decline in the number of whites or to achieve a permanently interracial neighborhood, one must create conditions that successfully encourage white immigration. As

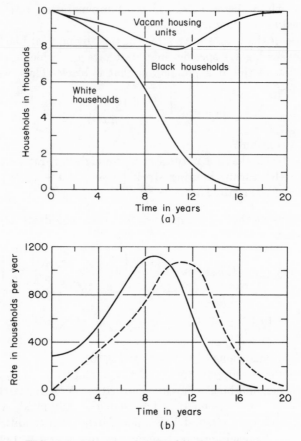

FIG. 2-4   Migration Amplified by Racial Friction

Equation (2-13) with $N = 10,000$, $\mu_m = 0.03$, $c_1 = c_2 = 0.5$. (a) Housing occupancy; (b) overall migration rates: ——, white rate, – – – black rate.

long as most immigrants are black and most emigrants are white, the model's results are inevitable.

2-6   Forrester's Urban Dynamics

At any one moment in time, an urban area might be described quite adequately by inventorying its population, capital and industries, land, transport system, utilities, and governmental operations. But if one wants to predict how one or more of these assets change with time, naturally or in response to imposed stimuli, one must model their effects upon one another as well as their interrelationships with the outside world. A bold, imaginative effort to this end was taken by Forrester in 1969. His book, *Urban Dynamics* [4], presents a time-dependent model, which describes the long-term development of an area by modeling the interactions among population, industry, and housing at a level of detail judiciously chosen to avoid onerous complication while still exhibiting many points of genuine interest.

Forrester's method consists of classifying business enterprises, housing, and population into a number of cohorts. The number of units or families in any one cohort at any time is called the *level* of that cohort. The levels change with time because individuals are born or die, or because they migrate into or out of the cohort. The birth and death equations that describe this process are called *rate equations* by Forrester because they define the rates at which cohort levels change with time. Any one rate of change may be a function of any or all of the cohort levels, the other rates of change, land availability, governmental behavior, and the external world.

In Forrester's original formulation, the urban system is structured into nine cohorts as follows:

(a)   *Three Cohorts of People*

Families are placed, according to the economic status of their bread-winners, into a "manager and professional" cohort, a "worker" cohort, and an "underemployed" cohort. Each cohort changes level as a result of natural births and deaths, of changes in fortune which causes flows from one cohort to another, and of migrations to and from the world outside the particular urban system being studied. The population levels are expressed in terms of numbers of workers; so the number of dependents per worker can be supplied as socioeconomic parameters, which may differ among cohorts.

(b)   *Three Cohorts of Housing*

Each people-cohort occupies a corresponding housing-cohort. Births, or new construction, can occur in each housing-cohort. The birth flow rate for manager housing is largely a function of the ratio between the level of managers and the level of manager housing units. For workers' housing, the birth flow rate is determined both by objective need and by public housing policies. Public funds are the only source of new housing for the underemployed. In addition, there are migrations, or flows, of the aging housing stock from the manager to the worker and, ultimately, to the underemployed housing-cohorts. Housing abandonments, or deaths, are assumed to occur only in the underemployed housing-cohort.

(c)   *Three Cohorts of Industry*

Called "new," "mature," and "declining" industry-cohorts, these also change levels by a birth–death–migration process. New industry is characterized by small firms with an exceptionally high proportion of managers and professionals among their employees. Births occur in the new industry-cohort at a rate that is a function of government incentives and of available resources in people and land. There are flows of firms from new industry to mature industry and from mature industry to declining industry. The mature industry-cohort is characterized by large firms and by a high ratio of workers to managers. Declining industry consists of smaller firms with a relatively high proportion of underemployed workers. Deaths occur only in the declining industry-cohort.

These nine cohorts reside on a fixed land area embedded in a limitless outside world. The outside world is assumed to be unaffected by the one urban system so that it is always able to supply or receive limitless flows of migrant people as circumstances change within the system.

It remains to formulate explicitly the birth, death, and migration rates for each of the nine cohorts. In order to test and experiment with his model, Forrester postulated the forms and parameters for his rate equations in a rather subjective manner, aided by a former mayor of Boston and by other experienced persons. However, it is possible, at least in principle, to develop and calibrate objectively verified rate equations, based on statistical analysis of past behavior in suitable observable environments.

Forrester's formulation consisted of literally hundreds of relationships, many tabulated rather than analytical. Hence he had no option other than that of programming his model for numerical solution on a digital computer. To this end, he used DYNAMO II, a well-known simulation language which is quite easy to use and read. A novel aspect of *Urban Dynamics* is that all mathematical statements are given directly in the DYNAMO II language. Because of this, we shall illustrate Forrester's rate-equation formulation approach with an example in DYNAMO II, as presented in his book. The considered illustration is the rate of immigration from the outside world into the underemployed cohort.

In DYNAMO II, time is broken up into equal-length increments. The points, or moments, in time, which separate these increments, are labeled 0, 1, 2,..., J, K, L,.... Thus, J, K, and L are used to label successive moments, while JK and KL are used to represent the time intervals from J to K and from K to L. The various levels, rates, and other functions are defined by letters or groups of letters. The following illustrations show how levels and rates are expressed as functions of time and how equations are formed:

U.K = the level, in number of breadwinners, of the underemployed cohort at time moment K.

U.L = the same level, one time interval later.

UA.KL = the arrival rate, in number of breadwinners per time interval, of immigrants from the outside world into the underemployed cohort, prevailing for the time interval from moment K to moment L.

If the underemployed cohort level were a function only of the underemployed arrival rate UA (this is not true), then the underemployed cohort rate equation would be

$$U.L = U.K + UA.KL.$$

This is the DYNAMO II equivalent of

$$U(t + \tau) \cong U(t) + \frac{dU(t)}{dt} \cdot \tau,$$

where τ is the time interval between moment K and moment L, and t is the time corresponding to moment K.

Forrester assumes that the underemployed arrival rate has the form

$$UA.KL = (U.K + L.K)(UAN)(AMMP.K),$$

where

L = worker cohort level,

UAN = a normalizing multiplier, supplied as a parameter by the user of the model, and

AMMP = "attractiveness for migration multiplier—perceived." This function will be defined later.

In words, the outside immigration rate into the underemployed cohort, during the interval KL, is the product of (1) the sum of the worker and underemployed cohort levels, (2) a scaling parameter, and (3) a migration attractiveness function.

It is appropriate to assume that there is a time lag between an objective change in actual attractiveness for migrants and the subsequent perception of that change by prospective migrants. This time lag is modeled as follows:

$$\mathtt{AMMP.K = AMMP.J + (AMM.J - AMMP.J)/AMMPT,}$$

where

    AMM = actual "attractiveness for migration multiplier," and
  AMMPT = "attractiveness for migration multiplier—perceived time lag" factor.

The classical mathematical expression for this is

$$\mathrm{AMMP}(t + \tau) \cong \mathrm{AMMP}(t) + \left[\frac{\mathrm{AMM}(t) - \mathrm{AMMP}(t)}{\mathrm{AMMPT}} \right].$$

Finally, AMM is defined as

$$\mathtt{AMM.K = (UAMM.K)(UHM.K)(PEM.K)(UJM.K)(UHPM.K)(AMF),}$$

where

  UAMM = "underemployed arrivals mobility factor," a tabulated function which increases with an increase in the rate at which underemployed breadwinners migrate from their cohort up to the worker cohort;

    UHM = "underemployed housing multiplier," a tabulated function which increases with the ratio of the underemployed housing level to the underemployed level;

    PEM = "public expenditure multiplier," a tabulated function which increases with per-capita governmental expenditure;

    UJM = "underemployed job multiplier," a tabulated function which increases with the number of jobs for the underemployed provided by the three industry-cohorts;

  UHPM = "underemployed housing program multiplier," a tabulated function which increases with the size of the public housing program; and

    AMF = a constant parameter, used for calibration of the model.

For a listing of the tabulated functions mentioned here and for the equivalent formulations describing the many other rates entering into the model, the reader is urged to refer to Forrester's original text.

Forrester illustrates his model's behavior over time under a variety of assumed government action plans such as slum clearance, worker education programs, public welfare programs, and industrial subsidies. It is evident, even from the minute extract above, that his conclusions are likely to be sensitive to the arbitrary forms assumed for defining flow rates. Even though his particular illustrative conclusions may be wrong, the approach is useful and has stimulated much emulative work.

As originally propounded, Forrester's model contains two especially troublesome assumptions:

(1) The model external world is not affected by what happens in the study area. Thus, the effects of a government program within the area are modeled meaningfully only if it is not tried simultaneously in many other places. In the real world, cities emulate one another: A program, designed to attract business or to discourage immigration by the poor, would, if successful, soon be counteracted by an adaptive external world.

(2) The study area has a given fixed land area so that, in the absence of government action, the model reaches a terminal equilibrium stage where further growth is not possible. Such a formulation does correspond to a politically bounded city. However, once the real city faces lack of space, growth continues outside and suburbs develop. As soon as these suburbs contain substantial numbers of people or businesses, assumption (1) is undermined because life in the suburbs closely interacts with events in the central city.

2-7 Conclusion

The material of this chapter is basic to much of the urban modeling methodology. Nevertheless, it is not, by itself, very useful in predicting population, either for a metropolitan area as a whole or for individual neighborhoods therein. The overall metropolitan area is affected critically by employment opportunities which, ultimately, govern migration between itself and competing places elsewhere. When one seeks to predict such migration quantitatively, one needs to model the regional economy much more thoroughly than possible with the Forrester model. The main ways to do this are shown in Chapter 3. In contrast, the development of a particular neighborhood depends heavily on its accessibility for commuters and its available building land, both in competition with equivalent resources in competing neighborhoods. Appropriate land-use models have been invented, and these will be exhibited in Chapter 4.

For further development of the mathematics for population analysis, see the texts by Keyfitz [5] and Bartlett [2]. The practical methodology for data collection, stratification of results, and forecasting is considered at length by Cox [3], Barclay [1], and Peterson [6].

PROBLEMS

If the birth and death equation is too complicated to solve analytically, a numerical approximation can be found by setting

$$\frac{d\bar{n}(t)}{dt} \cong \frac{\bar{n}(t + \Delta) - \bar{n}(t)}{\Delta},$$

where Δ is a relatively short time interval such as one year. This technique may be appropriate for Problems 1–4.

1. Magic Mountain Hospital is a state institution for long-term diseases such as advanced tuberculosis or syphilis. During 1970, there were 300 new admissions, 200 deaths, and 100 discharges of "cured" patients. The hospital population was 1000 at the end of 1970. A study of past trends reveals that the number of admissions does not vary significantly from year to year. However, the numbers of deaths and discharges appear to be proportional to the number of inmates, with the coefficients of proportionality varying with time. For the 1970s, it is estimated that the average per-capita death rate, in any year, will be 80% as great as in the year before. Similarly, the average discharge rate will be 110% as great as in the prior year. On the basis of these facts and hypotheses, estimate the hospital population at the end of 1980.

   (*Answer:* About 1200.)

2. Repeat Problem 1 with the modification that the per-capita discharge rate each year is 105% of the rate in the previous year.

   (*Answer:* About 1475. The result is seen to be extremely sensitive with respect to the numerical assumptions made in setting up the problem.)

3. Jerreby, Ltd., will construct the new town of "Mountain Woods" on a 500-acre potato farm. Mountain Woods will consist of 2000 houses, to be built at a rate of 500 per year until the project is completed. Based on experience at earlier Jerreby projects, the houses will be sold and occupied as soon as they are completed. At the time of initial occu-

pancy, the average household will consist of 3.0 persons, distributed as follows:

Age	Average number of persons per household
0–1	0.2
1–2	0.2
2–3	0.2
3–4	0.1
4–5	0.1
5–6	0.1
over 6	2.1

The households are thus seen to be composed of young families. Therefore, it is estimated that the birthrate per household per year will be 0.20 for the first 6 years at Mountain Woods. Estimate the number of children, living in Mountain Woods, who will reach the age of 5 during each of the first 10 years after construction begins. The data are required by the school board.

4. Using a consistent arbitrary methodology, the United States Census Bureau classifies people as having either urban or rural domiciles. Based on this classification, the United States population was 51.2% urban in 1920, 56.2% urban in 1930, 56.5% urban in 1940, 59.6% urban in 1950, and 63.0% urban in 1960. (Under a new classification scheme, the figure was 69.9% in 1960, and subsequent data are hard to compare.) Use the data of Table 2-1 and make appropriate assumptions to predict further migration from rural to urban areas during the period from 1960 to 2000.

5. This question is appropriate only if you are aware of a specific neighborhood whose racial composition is changing or has changed recently. Are the assumptions of the Section 2.5 illustration at least moderately appropriate to this neighborhood? How should they be changed to make the model more suitable?

6. Sketch out, in broad outline, a Forrester-type model for predicting the proportion of children who will attend parochial schools, rather than public schools, in a well-developed older suburb of a large city. Suppose that both school systems exist and that both are prepared to accept all children who apply. However, the parochial system is very short of money so, as enrollment increases, the apparent quality of education will decline unless fees are raised.

The study suburb has a steady stream of emigrants to more spacious new developments. Immigrants come largely from the older central city and, on the average, are somewhat poorer than the emigrants. The immigrants have a larger number of children per family. A significant proportion of the immigrants are expected to be Puerto Ricans. Assume that the immigrants' racial, religious, and economic distributions have already been forecast and are available as input parameters for your model.

REFERENCES

[1] Barclay, G. W., *Techniques of Population Analysis.* Wiley, New York, 1958.
[2] Bartlett, M. S., *Stochastic Population Models in Ecology and Epidemology.* Methuen, London and Wiley, New York, 1960.
[3] Cox, P. R., *Demography,* 4th ed. Cambridge Univ. Press, London and New York, 1970.
[4] Forrester, J., *Urban Dynamics.* MIT Press, Cambridge, Massachusetts, 1969.
[5] Keyfitz, N., *Introduction to the Mathematics of Population.* Addison-Wesley, Reading, Massachusetts, 1968.
[6] Peterson, W., *Population,* 2nd ed. Macmillan, New York, 1969.
[7] *Statistical Abstracts of the United States,* 86th and 92nd eds. US Govt. Printing Office, Washington D.C., 1965 and 1971.

Chapter *3*

Economy

This chapter presents some models appropriate to the description and forecasting of urban and regional economies. The most important and effective of these is "input–output analysis," Section 3-4, wherein an effort is made to account for all economic activity in some detail.

Unfortunately, thorough economic analysis is complicated, subtle, and, above all, very time-consuming and expensive. Therefore, the practical planner often must resort to shortcuts, such as assuming that his area will behave just like an area for which analysis has been performed by someone else. For example, if the United States Department of Commerce has made a forecast for the California food-processing industry, one might "step down" this forecast so as to apply it to the town of Sacramento. There is no need to apologize for such a practice. However, it should be obvious that one can have no idea of the quality of such a derivative forecast unless one understands its basic source. So it is important to learn about the basic research tools, such as input–output analysis, even if one does not use them directly.

3-1 Cause and Effect in Urban Development

Two starkly contrasting views can be taken of the causes for urban growth or decay. In one, ideal for a traditional society in equilibrium, the primary mechanism is the change in population resulting from births, deaths, and socially inspired migration. The economy is viewed as responding to and, hence, a function of the population and its available resources. The birth–death–migration model of the previous chapter is suitable for developing this argument.

The second view, exhibited in the present chapter, is that a locality's population is a function of available employment and income. It is best applied to rapidly changing areas where people are adventurous, not rooted to their places of birth, and thus ready to migrate at any time.

The melding of the two approaches, so as to describe realistically an intermediate society, is a difficult task for which there is not as yet a well-established theory. Perhaps Forrester's "urban dynamics" approach, Section 2-6, will prove to be sufficiently flexible to provide a basis for further development.

3-2   Components of Growth Model

The understanding of economic change in an urban area may be enhanced by a very simple division of the gross rate of change into three components. We illustrate with a linearized argument, giving the change in employment ΔE_{ij} for industry sector i, in area j, during a selected time interval. Let $E_{ij}(t_1)$ be the employment at the beginning of the time interval, and let $E_{ij}(t_2)$ be the employment at the end, so

$$E_{ij}(t_2) = E_{ij}(t_1) + \Delta E_{ij}.$$

Let

r = fractional growth, or decline, of total national employment during the selected time interval;

r_i = fractional growth, or decline, of total national industry i employment during the time interval; and

r_{ij} = fractional growth, or decline, of industry i employment in area j during the time interval.

Then ΔE_{ij} can be divided as follows:

$$\Delta E_{ij} = \Delta E_{ij}^{(N)} + \Delta E_{ij}^{(Ni)} + \Delta E_{ij}^{(ij)},$$

where

$\Delta E_{ij}^{(N)} = rE_{ij}(t_1)$

= change of industry i employment, in area j, ascribable to total national employment growth;

$$\Delta E_{ij}{}^{(Ni)} = (r_i - r)E_{ij}(t_1)$$

= change of industry i employment, in area j, ascribable to the difference between national and industry i employment growths;

$$\Delta E_{ij}{}^{(ij)} = (r_{ij} - r_i)E_{ij}(t_1)$$

= change of industry i employment, in area j, ascribable to the difference between industry i growth nationally and industry i growth locally.

As an illustration, suppose that industry i, in area j, is the electrical equipment and supplies industry in Middletown. If this industry's employment was 5000 in 1960 and 6000 in 1970, then the change in employment for the decade was

$$\Delta E_{ij} = E_{ij}(1970) - E_{ij}(1960) = 6000 - 5000 = 1000,$$

yielding a fractional growth of $r_{ij} = [\Delta E_{ij}/E_{ij}(1960)] = 0.2000$. The total United States employed civilian labor force was 65,778,000 in 1960 and 78,627,000 in 1970, yielding $r = 0.1953$. The United States electrical industry labor force was 1,467,000 in 1960 and 1,923,000 in 1970, or $r_i = 0.3108$. Thus, the three components of Middletown's electrical industry employment growth were

$$\Delta E_{ij}{}^{(N)} = rE_{ij}(1960) = (0.1953)(5000) = 977,$$

$$\Delta E_{ij}{}^{(Ni)} = (r_i - r)E_{ij}(1960) = (0.1155)(5000) = 577,$$

$$\Delta E_{ij}{}^{(ij)} = (r_{ij} - r_i)E_{ij}(1960) = (-0.1108)(5000) = -554.$$

So $\Delta E_{ij} = 977 + 577 - 554 = 1000$. Any one of these four numbers could have been deduced from the other three. It can be seen at once that Middletown's electrical equipment industry is in trouble, having a very substantial decline in employment *relative* to that which prevailed elsewhere in the industry.

The components of growth approach can be used to chart and forecast changes in the industry mix of an area and the consequent changes in the area's sources and scale of personal incomes. Unfortunately, one usually must make somewhat debilitating assumptions, of constancy or assumed change, regarding future industry and national growth rates. For further information, see Ashby [2].

3-3 Economic Base–Multiplier Model

In any urban area, there are likely to be industries that produce largely for export to the region, nation, or even the world. Other industries exist primarily to serve the local market. The export industries can be viewed as "basic" to the economic existence of the area, while the rest are, in a simplified sense, "service" industries, which are ultimately dependent on the scale and success of the basic industries.

There are cities, such as Pittsburgh with its steel industry, where the basic sectors certainly dominate the economy. Where this is the case, it may be reasonable to postulate that the overall economy's scale is proportional to the level of business done by the basic export industries. The economic base–multiplier methodology exploits this situation. In its simplest form, the total area employment is postulated to be a predictable multiple of the basic industry employment. Thus, for forecasting it is necessary only to

(a) conduct a historical analysis to obtain the trend in the "multiplier ratio" between total and basic employments, and

(b) obtain, exogenously, an estimate of future export demands for the basic industry products.

Suppose that

$Q(t)$ = total area employment or income at time t,

$Q_E(t)$ = employment or income in basic sectors at time t, and

$Q_S(t)$ = employment or income in the rest of the economy, called service sector for convenience, at time t.

The simplest hypothesis is that the total is proportional to the scale of the basic sector; so $Q(t) = mQ_E(t)$, where m is a constant multiplier. Since $Q(t) = Q_E(t) + Q_S(t)$,

$$m = 1 + [Q_S(t)/Q_E(t)].$$

If there is appropriate evidence, it may be desirable to make $m = m(t)$, a function of time.

Clearly this method is unsuitable for areas not dominated by their basic export industries. Thus, though appropriate to Detroit, the method is much weaker for New York and is quite useless for a large region such as the northeastern United States "megalopolis."

There are further difficulties. If the study area is very small, the model is likely to be unduly sensitive to assumed changes in the fortunes of its basic sectors. Further, it is difficult to fully separate export from nonexport activities, particularly in industries, such as banking or insurance, where the exports are relatively invisible. Nevertheless, the approach seems to be attractive and useful, particularly to transportation and land-use planners, who must have at least a minimal quantitative future employment model before they can make any sensible forecasts in their domains. Thus, the model has been used for transportation studies of Pittsburgh [14] and Denver [19].

3-4   Input–Output Models

Input–output analysis, developed by Leontief [10], is the name given to an accounting procedure wherein the output of each industry is set equal to the consumption of that industry's product by other industries and by ultimate consumers. Used as a planning device to forecast future development, it is particularly suitable for detecting and quantifying constraints (shortages) which may inhibit the achievement of desired goals.

(a)   *An Illustration*

Suppose that there are three industries with output rates of, respectively, x_1, x_2, x_3. The output rates are measured in units of value per unit time, typically dollars per year. The output of each industry is used by itself, by the other two industries, and by the rest of the world—which we shall call the "consumers."

Let a_{ij}, where $i = 1, 2, 3$ and $j = 1, 2, 3$, be the value of product i required as input to produce one dollar's worth of product j. Thus, since industry 3 has an output rate of x_3, it will require an input rate $a_{23}x_3$ of industry 2's product. Let y_i, where $i = 1, 2, 3$, be the rate at which the consumers absorb industry i's product. On the basis of these definitions, the output rate of each industry can be equated to the sum of the input rates for that industry's product:

$$x_i = \sum_{j=1}^{3} a_{ij}x_j + y_i, \qquad \text{for} \quad i = 1, 2, 3. \tag{3-1}$$

Equation (3-1) can be used to deduce the output rates x_i required to yield any required inputs y_i to consumers, provided that one knows all the a_{ij}'s. These a_{ij}'s, arranged in a two-dimensional table, are called the "technological matrix" for the system being modeled.

For illustration, let

$$\{a_{ij}\} = \begin{bmatrix} a_{11} & a_{12} & a_{13} \\ a_{21} & a_{22} & a_{23} \\ a_{31} & a_{32} & a_{33} \end{bmatrix} = \begin{bmatrix} 0.1 & 0.4 & 0.2 \\ 0.3 & 0 & 0.5 \\ 0.2 & 0.2 & 0.6 \end{bmatrix}$$

and let the consumers require output rates of $y_1 = \$1000$ per year, $y_2 = \$2000$ per year, and $y_3 = \$3000$ per year. Then the input–output equations (3-1) become

$$x_1 = 0.1x_1 + 0.4x_2 + 0.2x_3 + 1000$$

$$x_2 = 0.3x_1 \qquad\qquad + 0.5x_3 + 2000$$

$$x_3 = 0.2x_1 + 0.2x_2 + 0.6x_3 + 3000$$

with solution $x_1 = \$14,615$ per year, $x_2 = \$18,385$ per year, and $x_3 = \$24,000$ per year. All these are considerably bigger than the consumer requirements, a not uncommon situation. Similar results are found for the grouping of iron, coal, and railroad industries, whose interactions with one another and with the consumer are much favored for input–output model illustrations.

In real applications, labor often is viewed as an industry, so as to exhibit required employment levels consequent to any assumed consumer demands.

(b)   Regional Economy Model

Input–output models have been used to describe the economies of Chicago [8], Boston [12], Philadelphia [9], the "Northeast Corridor" [18], and New York. We exhibit here a skeletal version of a New York Metropolitan Area model devised by Berman [3]. The area's economy was divided into $N = 43$ industrial sectors. For each industry, the output is divided among the other industries, local consumers, government, and the "export" national market. Let

$x_i(t)$ = output rate of ith industry at time t,
$z_{ij}(t)$ = input rate to jth industry of ith industry product at time t,
$z_{ic}(t)$ = input rate to local consumers of ith industry product at time t,
$z_{ig}(t)$ = input rate to government of ith industry product at time t, and
$z_{in}(t)$ = input rate to national market of ith industry product at time t.

The basic input–output equations are

$$x_i(t) = \sum_{j=1}^{N} z_{ij}(t) + z_{ic}(t) + z_{ig}(t) + z_{in}(t), \qquad (3\text{-}2)$$

where $i = 1, 2, \ldots, N$. Industry j makes two types of purchases from industry i. The first kind is needed for its product and is, therefore, proportional to its output, with constant of proportionality a_{ij}. The constant a_{ij} is the value of industry output i required by industry j to produce one one dollar's worth of product j. The second kind of purchase occurs as the result of expansion by industry j and may be viewed as raw material for plant expansion. If industry j expands, purchases from industry i are assumed to be proportional to the rate of change of output by industry j, with constant of proportionality c_{ij}. Thus,

$$z_{ij}(t) = a_{ij}x_j(t) + c_{ij}\frac{dx_j(t)}{dt}. \qquad (3\text{-}3)$$

If industry j contracts, $dx_j(t)/dt < 0$. In this case, it is assumed that there are no capital purchases; so $c_{ij} = 0$. If information is at hand regarding the change, with time, of the technological coefficients a_{ij} and c_{ij}, then one can appropriately make $a_{ij} = a_{ij}(t)$ and $c_{ij} = c_{ij}(t)$.

To ease computation, the derivative in Eq. (3-3) is replaced by a difference:

$$\frac{dx_j(t)}{dt} \cong \frac{x_j(t) - x_j(t - \Delta)}{\Delta}. \qquad (3\text{-}4)$$

The time interval Δ may be made one year, or shorter if there is reason to suppose that increased accuracy would be achieved.

Let $P(t)$ be the local area population and let $y(t)$ be the aggregate local personal income rate, both at time t. Consumer purchases are assumed to be proportional to $P(t)$ and to $y(t)$, with constants of proportionality m_i and f_i; so

$$z_{ic}(t) = m_iP(t) + f_iy(t). \qquad (3\text{-}5)$$

Government purchases are assumed to depend on population with

$$z_{ig}(t) = a_{ig}(t)P(t) + b_{ig}(t). \qquad (3\text{-}6)$$

The parameters $a_{ig}(t)$ and $b_{ig}(t)$ are made functions of time so that the researcher can study the effects of time-variant government policies.

By substituting Eqs. (3-3) to (3-6) into Eq. (3-2), one obtains

$$x_i(t) = \sum_{j=1}^{N} [(a_{ij} + c_{ij}/\Delta) x_j(t) - (c_{ij}/\Delta) x_j(t - \Delta)]$$

$$+ [m_i + a_{ig}(t)] P(t) + f_i y(t) + b_{ig}(t) + z_{in}(t). \quad (3\text{-}7)$$

The national market purchases, $z_{in}(t)$, must be estimated exogenously to the model, perhaps from a national input–output model. If these are at hand, one has N equations, (3-7), with $(N + 2)$ unknowns, consisting of $x_1(t)$, $x_2(t),\ldots,$ $x_N(t)$, $P(t)$, and $y(t)$. It remains to express $P(t)$ and $y(t)$ as functions of employment and to express employment as a function of production. Let

$$E(t) = \text{total local area employment at time } t,$$

$e_j(t), e_g(t), e_h(t) = $ local area employment in industry j, in government, and in private households at time t.

Assume that

$$e_j(t) = h_j(t) x_j(t), \qquad e_g(t) = q(t) P(t) + s(t),$$

and that $e_h(t)$ is estimated independently of the model. The parameter $h_j(t)$ is the number of employees per unit production rate in industry j. One must estimate $q(t)$ and $s(t)$, both of which are the result of time-varying public policy. Then

$$E(t) = \sum_{j=1}^{N} e_j(t) + e_g(t) + e_h(t)$$

$$= \sum_{j=1}^{N} h_j(t) x_j(t) + q(t) P(t) + s(t) + e_h(t). \quad (3\text{-}8)$$

Finally, population and total personal income are made proportional to employment,

$$P(t) = g(t) E(t) \qquad \text{and} \qquad y(t) = k(t) E(t), \quad (3\text{-}9)$$

where $g(t)$ and $y(t)$, perhaps not varying much with time, must be estimated exogenously to the model.

The N equations (3-7) plus the one equation (3-8) constitute $(N + 1)$ equations in $(N + 1)$ unknowns $x_1(t)$, $x_2(t),\ldots,$ $x_N(t)$, and $E(t)$. After all the parameters are estimated, these equations can be solved successively for moments separated by the equal time increments Δ. The solution is likely to be an enormous undertaking, requiring the use of a high-speed computer and critically dependent on the validities of the several simplifying assumptions made in the formulation.

The New York area study, which used this model, was reported in detail by Lichtenberg [13] before sufficient time had passed to establish the validity of the results. Now, some years later, it appears that some of the forecasts made were quite inaccurate. There were two main difficulties. First, the model appears to be unable to cope successfully with declining industries. Second, the New York area is most dependent on such invisible exports as corporate management, insurance, and banking. These seem to pose special difficulties in calibration and interpretation. Nevertheless, the input–output formalism seems to be the best available for analyzing a regional economy.

(c) Calibration Problems

The regional input–output model will not be operational until the technological coefficients a_{ij} and c_{ij} are evaluated with satisfactory accuracy. It should be recalled that a_{ij} is the value of industry product i required for a unit value output by industry j, and that c_{ij} is the value of industry product i required for a unit value increase in industry j's output capacity.

For the United States national economy, these coefficients have been worked out with great care and are readily available for incorporation into local models; one good source is Reference [1]. But the coefficients are likely to be different for any one particular locality because:

(1) The local industries may not be typical in their input demands. They use locally appropriate processes, conditioned by the local cost structure for materials, utilities, and labor. This cost structure may differ significantly from the national average.

(2) While technology changes constantly with time, the averaged national changes are likely to be gradual and susceptible to useful extrapolation. However, in a small area, such changes can be abrupt and unpredictable.

(3) The national economy's imports and exports are closely monitored and thus are fully known quantities. This is not the case locally, and it is difficult to separate locally purchased inputs from inputs imported from outside the area. But the a_{ij}'s and c_{ij}'s are supposed to reflect only the *local* portions of the technology matrices.

While corrections can be made to partially overcome these difficulties, there is no really adequate substitute for fully developed local data obtained directly by surveys of local economic activity.

Reference [16] offers a good review, with complete bibliography, of these and other considerations and of the state of the art (1972) in coping with them.

3-5   Economy and the Quality of Urban Life

Input–output analysis is a good tool for estimating the environmental and personal amenity effects of inevitable or planned developments in the economy. As suggested by Hirsch *et al.* [7], the gross urban environment can be divided into several systems: the natural, the community services, the community infrastructure, the sociocultural, and the economic. The problem is to show the economy's effects on the individual's environment both directly and indirectly, the latter through its effects on the other environmental systems.

The basic regional input–output model aggregates the society's participation into gross household income and gross government "welfare" expenditure. Real insight, into the economic environment of individuals, can be obtained only if household incomes are divided into several sectors, according to level of prosperity, and if government expenditure is divided into functionally stratified sectors such as education, health, personal income maintenance, public safety, fire fighting, recreation, transit, water supply, and sanitation. If the input–output model is thus stratified, one can begin to deduce who is making what kind of expenditure, given any level and mix of economic activity in an area.

Those urban systems that have performance indices not normally expressed in economic terms can be tied to the economic model in at least two ways. The first is to develop individual relationships, or "linkages," between particular economic activities and the affected systems. For example, the relation between steel output and particulate emissions into the atmosphere can thus be expressed and studied. However, a more complete analysis can be made by using a "dummy sector" approach, wherein the additional activities are treated in the same way as are the basic industrial sectors. With this approach, one would postulate a dummy "atmospheric particulate matter" industrial sector, one of whose inputs would be the steel industry. The input–output mechanism then provides a way to exhibit both the inputs and the (undesired) outputs of this dummy sector.

Leontief and Ford [11] have applied a version of the dummy sector approach to the general analysis of the effects of air pollution. The original industry sectors, $i = 1, 2, \ldots, N$, are expanded by antipollution activity sectors $g = N + 1, N + 2, \ldots, M$, one for each pollutant of concern. Input and output rates are defined as follows:

x_i = output rate of industry i.

x_g = output of antipollution activity sector g, expressed as the rate at which pollutant g is *reduced*.

r_g = rate at which pollutant g is released to pollute the air. This is equal to the rate at which the pollutant is produced minus the rate at which it is reduced by the antipollution effort.

y_i = input rate of industry product i to consumers, government, and export markets.

The technological coefficients are:

a_{ij} = input of product i required for a unit output of product j.

a_{ig} = input of product i required for a unit reduction in pollutant g.

a_{gi} = output of pollutant g per unit output of product i.

a_{gk} = output of pollutant g resulting from a unit reduction in pollutant k.

In the above, $i, j = 1, 2, \ldots, N$, and $g, k = N + 1, N + 2, \ldots, M$. The input–output equations are

$$x_i = \sum_{j=1}^{N} a_{ij} x_j + \sum_{g=N+1}^{M} a_{ig} x_g + y_i \qquad \text{for} \quad i = 1, 2, \ldots, N \qquad (3\text{-}10\text{a})$$

$$x_g + r_g = \sum_{i=1}^{N} a_{gi} x_i + \sum_{k=N+1}^{M} a_{gk} x_k \qquad \text{for} \quad g = N + 1, \ldots, M. \quad (3\text{-}10\text{b})$$

Equations (3-10a) equate the output of each industry to the inputs of other industries, of pollution reduction activities, and of consumers. Equations (3-10b) state that the atmosphere and the pollution reduction activities absorb all the pollutants produced by the industry sectors and by the pollution-reducing activities. The pollution reducing activities are included as potential polluters because the mechanism for reducing one pollutant may produce others as by-products.

If v_i is the value added to the economy by a unit output of product i, and if v_g is the imputed value added to the economy by a unit reduction in pollutant g, then the value of the overall economic output is

$$V = \sum_{i=1}^{N} v_i x_i + \sum_{g=N+1}^{M} v_g x_g. \qquad (3\text{-}11)$$

The economic impact of an air pollution eliminating activity can be evaluated by finding V both with and without that activity. Note that the coefficients v_i and v_g really are not constants because there are diminishing returns as the scale of production increases. But if the changes caused by a pollution control activity are not very large, one may assume that these are constant over the output range actually considered. A more serious problem arises in the evaluation of v_g because the secondary economic effects of pollution are matters of public disagreement. If one assigns to v_g only directly measurable costs of the pollutant, one rather under-estimates the value of any clean air program.

Leontief and Ford applied this model to estimate the changes in costs, and consequent changes in the price structure, which would result from a complete implementation of the United States Clean Air Act of 1967.

3-6 Conclusion

In seeking to present a concise introduction, this chapter has glossed over most of the difficulties in data collection and model calibration that arise inevitably in quantitative economic analysis. For further information, Miernyk [15] is recommended as a good general text on the input–output methodology, and Boudeville [4] and Nourse [17] are recommended for reading on regional economic modeling.

REFERENCES

[1] Almon, C. *The American Economy to 1975*. Harper, New York, 1966.
[2] Ashby, L. D., *Regional Change in a National Economy*, Staff Working Paper No. 7. US Dept. of Commerce, Washington, D.C., 1964.
[3] Berman, B., Hoover, E. M., and Chinitz, B., *Technical Supplement to the New York Metropolitan Regional Study*. Harvard Univ. Press, Cambridge, Massachusetts, 1961.
[4] Boudeville, J. R., *Problems of Regional Planning*. Edinburgh Univ. Press, Edinburgh, Scotland, 1967.
[5] Carter, A. P., and Brody, A., ed., Vol. 1, Contributions to input-output analysis, Vol. 2, Applications of input-output analysis. *Proc. Int. Conf. on Input-Output Techniques, 4th, 1968*. Amer. Elsevier, New York, 1972.
[6] Carter, A. P., and Brody, A., ed., *Input-Output Techniques*. North-Holland Publ., Amsterdam and Amer. Elsevier, New York, 1972.
[7] Hirsch, W. Z., Sonenblum, S., and St. Denis, J., Estimating the quality of urban life with input-output. In *Input-Output Techniques* (A. P. Carter and A. Brody, eds.), pp. 44–62. North-Holland Publ., Amsterdam and Amer. Elsevier, New York, 1972.
[8] Hoch, I., Economic Activity Forecast. Final Rep. Chicago Area Transportation Study, Chicago, Illinois, 1959.
[9] Isard, W., Langford, T. W., and Romanoff, E., *Philadelphia Regional Input-Output Study: Working Papers*, Vols. 1–4, Regional Sci. Res. Inst., Philadelphia, Pennsylvania, 1966–1968.
[10] Leontief, W., *et al.*, *Studies in the Structure of the American Economy*. Oxford Univ. Press, London and New York, 1953.

[11] Leontief, W., and Ford, D. Air pollution and the economic structure: Empirical results of input-output computations. In *Input-Output Techniques* (A.P. Carter and A. Brody, eds.), pp. 9–30. North-Holland Publ., Amsterdam and Amer. Elsevier, New York, 1972.

[12] Leven, C. L., Legler, J. B., and Shapiro, P., *An Analytical Framework for Regional Development Policy*. MIT Press, Cambridge, Massachusetts, 1970.

[13] Lichtenberg, R. M., *One Tenth of a Nation*. Harvard Univ. Press, Cambridge, Massachusetts, 1960.

[14] Lowry, I. S., *A Model of Metropolis*. Rand Corp., Santa Monica, California, 1964.

[15] Miernyk, W. H., *The Elements of Input-Output Analysis*. Random House, New York, 1965.

[16] Miernyk, W. H., Regional and Interregional input-output models: A reappraisal. *Spatial, Regional and Population Economics* (M. Perlman, C. J. Leven, and B. Chinitz, eds.), pp. 263–292. Gordon & Breach, New York, 1972.

[17] Nourse, H. O., *Regional Economics*. McGraw-Hill, New York, 1968.

[18] Putnam, S. H., Analytic models for implementing the economic impact studies for the northeast corridor transportation project. CONSAD Res. Corp., Pittsburgh, Pennsylvania, 1966.

[19] *Working Denver*. City of Denver Planning Office, Denver, Colorado, 1953.

Chapter 4

Land and Its Development

4-1 Land-Use Forecasting

The term "land-use forecasting" is applied to the prediction of spatial distributions for residences, commercial establishments, and industry. For historical and psychological reasons, virtually all work has been directed at forecasting growth in the intensity and extent of urban land use. There is at present no tested methodology for predicting the decline of population densities in the inner parts of older cities, even though such declines are commonplace responses to increasing real personal wealth and the mobility conferred by widespread automobile ownership.

Land-use forecasts are needed for the effective location and scaling of transportation systems, public utilities, schools, hospitals, and commercial establishments. In addition, they are needed by government to help establish "zoning" rules on where and at what scale new development is to be permitted and encouraged.

A household or business, when seeking a location for its home, applies many criteria to the decision process of choosing a particular location in preference to others which are available concurrently. Clearly, the site finally chosen is one that has the greatest value, or utility, as measured subjectively by the new occupant. He is constrained in his choice by his financial resources and by the locations he must reach (or be reachable from) in daily life. All other things being equal, he is likely to choose the same neighborhood already settled by his peers. Thus it is agreed generally that the chief predictors, of the likelihood that a particular neighborhood is chosen, are:

(a)   The existing settlement of that neighborhood and the presently observed settlement pattern there.

(b)   The number of suitable vacant development sites in that neighborhood.

(c)   The cost of reaching, or being reached from, those places that must be accessible on a daily basis. This cost is most commonly measured in units of travel time by the predominant available mode of transportation. Sometimes more elegant cost functions are formulated to include travel time, money cost, and measures of comfort, reliability, and even social status of available travel modes.

(d)   The actual purchase or rent cost of the available sites, as viewed in the context of the potential user's resources and his alternate options.

In principle, all these predictors ought to be used in a land-use forecasting model. Yet all but (a) present serious formulation or calibration difficulties:

(b')   The number of suitable vacant sites in a neighborhood may be changed substantially by a change in zoning regulations. Such a change in the ground rules may well be spurred by the observed actual settlement pattern early during the prediction time horizon. It may even come about as a result of the forecast by itself. For example, rapid development of a suburban area may spur the older residents to enact a change in minimum residential lot size from $\frac{1}{2}$ acre to 2 acres, thus reducing the number of sites by 75%. On the whole, the pragmatic modeler ignores this problem as being beyond his competence. He proposes to use the best available estimates on the number of vacant sites and is prepared to repeat his analysis for alternative zoning plans.

(c')   The travel time associated with any neighborhood will be changed by changes in the transportation system that serves the neighborhood. Since such changes inevitably are made in response to actual or predicted land-use changes, there is an unavoidable interaction between land development and the transportation system. Models actually used have not coped directly with this interaction. The view taken is that one ought to develop the best possible decoupled models for land development in a given transport environment and for the transportation system for a given land-use pattern. Then the coupling of the two can be effected by an iterative application of the two models alternatively until their premises and forecasts are consistent.

(d')   It is very difficult to obtain and organize the data necessary for modeling the land market well enough to predict even roughly the relative utilities of all available land sites as viewed by the potential users of land. Consequently, the majority of land-use analysts have ignored this aspect or, at most, have made mild obeisance to it by predicting separately the land choices for economically disparate cohorts.

The simplest land-use models extrapolate past population trends, use only predictors (a) and (b), and thus suffer from being incapable of forecasting the effects of changes in the transport system. Somewhat more sophisticated are travel-time-oriented models which, in their basic forms, use only predictors (b) and (c). Two of these, the "gravity" model and the "intervening opportunity" model, have been widely used by transportation planners who have found them useful though not admirably accurate. At least one model—cluster, opportunity, and trend (COT)—has sought to use predictors (a), (b), and (c) together. There have been a number of land market modeling efforts that have seriously used (d) in addition to one or more of the other predictor inputs.

To simplify discussion, the models will be described in the context of residential land-use forecasting. Though the model forms can be adapted to industrial and commercial development, it ought to be pointed out that, in these areas, they are likely to be less successful. The models generally have a probabilistic approach, focused on the average behavior of a large number of individuals. Business enterprises are fewer in number than households and, further, tend to have very individualistic land requirements and zoning problems.

In a prosperous society, people live in the bedrooms of housing units built for residential use. The people redistribute themselves substantially only after additional bedrooms are constructed to receive them. Thus, the primary problem in the prediction of the population's spatial distribution is the one of predicting where the new housing units will be built. An additional room can be built only on a site not yet occupied by a room; replacement housing does not affect the overall population distribution. Thus the first requirement in urban growth prediction is to locate and enumerate all vacant sites suitable and legal for housing. For any given area, the available number of sites is the maximum number minus the number already built there.

The distribution of available vacant sites changes as the city develops. Areas near the centroid will tend toward saturation with few remaining opportunities for further development. The suburbs will become more and more attractive simply because uncommitted sites of reasonable size will be more numerous there. The order of accessibility may be changed, usually in favor of the suburbs, by new transport facilities and by rezoning in the more crowded areas.

4-2 Modeling Framework

Unless stated otherwise, the models described in this chapter seek to predict the spatial distribution of households, given the total population of households, as a function of time for the area as a whole.

The area to be modeled is given a precisely specified boundary. The interior is divided into a number of *zones*. Ideally, each zone is small enough to have a single predominant land use, such as residences, office buildings, parkland, retail commerce, or factories. Further, a zone ought to be small enough so a single point, called the *zone centroid*, can be used in establishing reasonably accurate travel time between points within the zone and points in all other zones. Generally, one cannot make zones so ideally small because then the study area would have more zones than one could afford to analyze. Typical compromises divide an urban area into somewhere between 10 and 1000 zones, with boundaries chosen to correspond to the boundaries of census tracts; so the study can have the full data benefits of standard census enumerations.

The world outside the study area is divided into one or more *external zones* and is analyzed quite sketchily.

Because almost all urban areas have one or more central business districts (often called CBDs), it is useful to set one characteristic location, called *high-value corner* (HVC), for each central business district. Then the travel time from any point to the central business district is taken to be the time from that point's zone centroid to the high-value corner.

In residential land-use modeling, the unit of population is the household, and the unit of land is the household site. The number of household sites usually is poorly correlated with the physical area of a zone because land-use rules or customs can result in occupancies as high as 500 households per acre at the centers of old crowded cities and as low as 1 household per 10 acres in some particularly wealthy and exclusive suburbs.

4-3 A Trend Model

The simplest possible extrapolation of past trends is the assignment of total population increase among the zones in such a way that each zone gets the same proportion of future growth that it was observed to get during a given period just past. Thus if there are N zones, if the total population growth (or decline) in a just past period was Δp, and if the growth of zone i in the same period was Δp_i, then let

$$g_i = \frac{\Delta p_i}{\Delta p} = \text{fraction of growth (or decline) to be assigned to zone } i,$$

$$\text{where} \quad i = 1, 2, \ldots, R.$$

An exogenously estimated future total growth of ΔP would then be distributed among zones on the basis that

$$\Delta P_i = g_i \, \Delta P = \text{predicted population growth in zone } i.$$

The immediately evident weakness in this approach is that one might assign a greater number of households to a zone than that zone has room for. This difficulty is perhaps best overcome by first distributing the population according to past trends, as above, and then performing one or more reassignments on the principle that the proportion of available sites used should vary fairly smoothly as one proceeds from the crowded city center to the sparsely populated outer zones. Though this approach has an element of qualitative judgment entering what a purist would prefer to be an entirely "mathematical" model, it has been used with some success in the Chicago Area Transportation Study [9]. It is known as the "density saturation gradient model."

Pure population trend models have fallen out of favor because

(1) they cannot show the effects of changes in the transportation network, and

(2) they cannot forecast meaningful population changes for zones that initially have a very small population.

4-4   Gravity Model

The gravity model, sometimes called the accessibility model, postulates that the likelihood of building on a site in a given zone is largely a function of the zone's distance or travel time from places of employment or commerce. While the origin of this much used approach is not clearly documented, an early effort by Hanson [10] certainly deserves major credit.

(a)   Formulation

Let $N(t)$ be the number of housing units in the study area, expressed as a function of time. It is assumed that this quantity is known or is estimated by means other than the gravity model. Let $g(t) = dN(t)/dt$ be the rate of growth in the number of housing units. As normally used, the model requires that

(a) $g(t) \geq 0$ at all times, and

(b)   there is nearly 100% housing unit occupancy so that the concepts of housing units and households are readily interchangeable.

The gravity model seeks to allocate the growth rate $g(t)$ among the R zones of the study area. The growth rate $g_i(t)$ for zone i, where $i = 1, 2, \ldots, R$, is set as proportional to the product of

$V_i(t)$ = the number of vacant housing sites in zone i, and

$A_i(t)$ = the accessibility index of zone i, about which more will be said below. For the present, note only that $A_i(t)$ will be large for a preferred location and small for a bad location.

Thus,

$$g_i(t) = C(t)V_i(t)A_i(t) \qquad \text{for} \quad i = 1, 2, \ldots, R. \qquad (4\text{-}1)$$

The time-dependent "constant" of proportionality $C(t)$ must be chosen so that the sum of the zone growth rates is equal to the exogenously determined total growth rate $g(t)$:

$$g(t) = \sum_{j=1}^{R} g_j(t). \qquad (4\text{-}2)$$

If one sums Eq. (4-1) over all R zones and substitutes $g(t)$ from Eq. (4-2), one finds

$$C(t) = \frac{g(t)}{\displaystyle\sum_{j=1}^{R} V_j(t)A_j(t)}$$

so

$$g_i(t) = g(t) \left[\frac{V_i(t)A_i(t)}{\displaystyle\sum_{j=1}^{R} V_j(t)A_j(t)} \right]. \qquad (4\text{-}3)$$

This is the gravity model in a form commonly used for land-use forecasting. The model is used to forecast $N_i(t)$, the number of housing units or households, in zone i at time t, given the following information:

(a) $N_i(t = 0) = N_i(0)$.

(b) $V_i(t = 0) = V_i(0) =$ number of vacant housing sites in zone i at time zero.

(c) $g(t) =$ total growth rate for the study area as a function of time.

(d) $A_i(t) =$ accessibility index of zone i at time t.

Note that

$$\frac{dN_i(t)}{dt} = g_i(t) \qquad (4\text{-}4)$$

and that

$$V_i(t) = V_i(0) - [N_i(t) - N_i(0)]. \qquad (4\text{-}5)$$

Substitution of Eqs. (4-4) and (4-5) into Eq. (4-3) yields

$$\frac{dN_i(t)}{dt} = g(t) \left\{ \frac{[V_i(0) + N_i(0) - N_i(t)]A_i(t)}{\sum_{j=1}^{R} [V_j(0) + N_j(0) - N_j(t)]A_j(t)} \right\} ; \qquad (4\text{-}6)$$

so

$$N_i(t) = N_i(0) + \int_0^t \frac{dN_i(t')}{dt'} \, dt'. \qquad (4\text{-}7)$$

It is normal practice to divide time into increments of Δt, typically one year, and to replace the differential equations (4.6) and (4-7) by the difference equations

$$\Delta N_i(t) = [\text{right-hand side of Eq. (4-6)}] \cdot \Delta t;$$

so

$$N_i(t + \Delta t) = N_i(t) + \Delta N_i.$$

(b)   Calibration

When the gravity model was first used, it was hoped that the accessibility index $A_i(t)$ might be expressed as a very simple analytic function of travel time $d_{ci}(t)$ between the study area center and the centroid of zone i. The form tried was

$$A_i(t) = \frac{1}{[d_{ci}(t)]^b},\qquad(4\text{-}8)$$

where b was to be a number, $b > 0$, obtained by calibration on past residential settlement patterns. The formalism was christened "gravity model" because substitution of Eq. (4-8) into Eq. (4-1), with $b = 2$, yields an equation much like Newton's gravitational force equation. In this case, $V_i(t)$ can be viewed as the "mass" of zone i.

It was found that the gravity model is not a good land-use predictor when $A_i(t)$ is made to take the simple form (4-8). However, rather good calibration results were obtained by assuming that $A_i(t)$ is a function *only* of the travel time $d_{ci}(t)$ to the center, though the functions found by calibration on this basis were much messier than Eq. (4-8).

The assumption that the *form* of the relation between $A_i(t)$ and $d_{ci}(t)$ does not itself depend on time makes it possible to deduce this relation from past growth patterns and then use it for predicting the future.

There is no computational difficulty if only one time interval is used to calibrate the study area model. Suppose that growth data are at hand for the time interval $(t_0, t_0 + \Delta t)$ in the form of numbers for

$g_i(t_0)\,\Delta t$ = number of new housing units constructed in zone i during the given time interval,

$V_i(t_0)$ = number of vacant housing sites in zone i at time t_0, and

$d_{ci}(t_0)$ = travel time between the study area center and the centroid of zone i at time t_0.

Then, by Eq. (4-1),

$$[C(t_0)\,\Delta t] \cdot A_i(t_0) \cong \left[\frac{g_i(t_0)\,\Delta t}{V_i(t_0)}\right].$$

One may set $C(t_0)\,\Delta t = 1$ because normalization for the $A_i(t)$ will be provided automatically by the gravity model, Eq. (4-3), when used for prediction. Therefore, let

$$A_i{}^*(t_0) = [C(t_0)\,\Delta t] \cdot A_i(t_0) = \left[\frac{g_i(t_0)\,\Delta t}{V_i(t_0)}\right].\qquad(4\text{-}9)$$

The procedure now is to calculate the $A_i{}^*(t_0)$ for all i and to plot the values found as functions of the corresponding $d_{ci}(t_0)$. A curve is fitted to the points obtained by means of the least-squares method, or otherwise. This curve then represents the relationship between accessibility $A_i{}^*$ and travel

TABLE 4-1
Gravity Model Calibration—Illustrative Example[a]

Zone Number i	$d_{ci}(t_0)$ (minutes)	$V_i(t_0)$	$g_i(t_0)\,\Delta t$	$A_i^* = \dfrac{g_i(t_0)\,\Delta t}{V_i(t_0)}$
1	3	1000	200	0.20
2	5	1000	60	0.06
3	5	1000	100	0.10
4	6	1000	70	0.07
5	8	1000	50	0.05
6	12	1000	20	0.02
7	13	1000	30	0.03
8	15	1000	10	0.01
9	20	1000	10	0.01
10	25	1000	10	0.01

[a] $t_0 = 1970$; $\Delta t =$ one year.

time d_{ci}. The relation is presumed time independent and is used for prediction.

The above procedure is illustrated by Table 4-1, wherein fictional 1970 data are developed for an $R = 10$ zone area. The results are shown in Fig. 4-1.

It should be noted that this procedure is valid only when just one set of data is used for calibration. Recall that $C(t_0)\,\Delta t$ was arbitrarily set equal to 1 and that any other positive constant would have served as well. A second, independent calibration, based on a different time period or a different time interval, would have the A^*'s scaled differently as a result of its $C(t_0)\,\Delta t'$ being set equal to 1. The two sets of A^* will require some manipulation to bring them to the same scale if they are to be averaged.

A considerably more elegant approach to developing an accessibility index is to suppose that the index for zone i is the sum of R terms, one for each zone, in the form

$$A_i(t) = \sum_{j=1}^{R} E_j(t) F_{ij}(t), \qquad (4\text{-}10)$$

where E_j is a measure of the attractive activity in zone j, such as total employment, and $F_{ij}(t)$ is a measure of "friction" or accessibility between zones i and j. Clearly, $F_{ij}(t)$ might be assumed to be a function only of the travel time between the centroids of zones i and j.

Calibration of the $F_{ij}(t)$ can be done in a manner analogous to that shown for the simpler case above. However, because a study area is likely

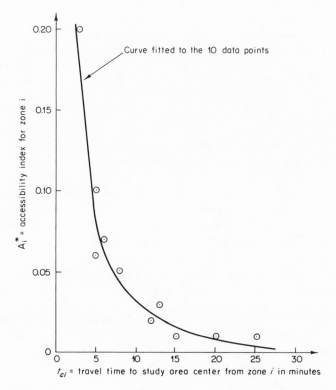

FIG. 4-1   Gravity Model Calibration—Illustrative Example

to be divided into hundreds of zones, there may be tens of thousands F_{ij}'s to evaluate. Thus, a digital computer may prove to be most useful. The United States Bureau of Public Roads has prepared a gravity model calibration program for the IBM 7090/7094 computer series [3]. Though intended for trip distribution, which is discussed in the next chapter, the program can be adapted to land-use forecasting.

(c)   The Lowry Model

The basic gravity model, applied to households, predicts residential locations on the basis of their accessibilities to the center, or centers, of employment. However, a large fraction of employment is in the service industries that are residence oriented, such as retail trade. These industries locate themselves on the basis of where their customers live. Thus, there is reason to augment the residential location model with an interacting employment location model. This has been done by Lowry [19], who developed his formalism by application to land-use forecasting in the Pittsburgh metropolitan area. The Lowry model has been the basis for further studies of Pittsburgh [4], the San Francisco Bay area [8], and several regions in Great Britain [5, 6].

In the Lowry model, employment is divided into two main classes, "basic" and "population serving." The locations of basic employment are determined exogenously to the model. In Pittsburgh the main basic industry is steel, whose locational criteria emphasize access to bulk transportation, suitable space, and contiguity to interrelated activities. The locations of those households supported by the basic employment are modeled by a gravity formalism. Then, given the predicted residence locations of basic industry households, the locations of service employment are forecast for the level of service required by these households. The service industries are divided into three categories—neighborhood, local, and metropolitan—and a separately calibrated gravity-type model is used for each category.

Then the residential household location model is used again, now to forecast the home locations for the service employees' households. The process is repeated: The service employees' residences also require services; so another increment of service employment is generated and located with regard to their residences. Household locations are forecast for this new increment of employees. The iteration stops when the number of households still to be assigned becomes very small.

It is assumed that, having greater economic strength, employment locations have priority over residences in any zone where there are insufficient sites for all employment or residential units that would settle there if space were ample.

4-5 Intervening Opportunity Model

This model, invented by Stouffer [25] for predicting the distribution of residential housing, is based on the assumption that the probability of building a new housing unit on a vacant site is a monotonically decreasing function of the number of equivalent vacant sites nearer than it to the centroid of all such sites.

The basic hypothesis is that a builder first considers the most accessible vacant site. There is some probability that he accepts it. If not, he considers the next most accessible site. If this is not accepted, he proceeds outward until he does accept a site.

The hierarchy of vacant site opportunities is likely to differ for different socioeconomic classes. Thus, the model may have to be worked out separately for each of several such classes. It should be pointed out, however, that in the United States today almost all new site construction is for relatively prosperous people. Though there is some new housing for the poor, this is mostly in the form of redevelopment of already committed land.

(b) Formulation

For simplicity, the model is presented first in a time-independent form, wherein it is assumed that all housing units are built at the same moment.

Let all vacant housing sites in the area be ordered so that the most accessible one is the first, the second most accessible one is the second, and so forth. The vacant sites can thus be described by the set of integers $1, 2, \ldots, m, \ldots$. No last integer need be specified since the number of conceivable sites is usually very large compared to the number that will actually be used.

Consider the selection of one housing site for subsequent construction of a housing unit. The site selector is assumed to consider the first site and to accept it, with probability P, or reject it, with probability $(1 - P)$. If the first site is rejected, the second is considered in the same manner. The process is repeated until a site is accepted. Thus, P is the probability of accepting any site m, given that the more accessible $(m - 1)$ sites have been rejected. For the present, P is viewed as a constant parameter.

Because sites are numerous, integer-valued m is viewed as a continuous variable. Let dm be the number of sites between m and $m + dm$. Then Pdm is the probability that a housing site is selected in the range dm, given that it was not selected in the better site range between zero and m. Let $\Pr(m)$ be the probability that the site selected will be less accessible than the m most accessible sites. Then $\Pr(m + dm)$, the probability of not accepting the first $(m + dm)$ sites, is the product of

(a)   the probability $\Pr(m)$ of not accepting the first m sites, and
(b)   the probability $\Pr(1 - Pdm)$ of *not* accepting a site in the range dm.

Mathematically,

$$\Pr(m + dm) = \Pr(m)(1 - Pdm). \tag{4-11}$$

Rearrange Eq. (4-11),

$$\frac{\Pr(m + dm) - \Pr(m)}{dm} = -P \Pr(m), \qquad (4\text{-}12)$$

and note that, in the limit as dm approaches zero, the left-hand side of Eq. (4-12) becomes $d \Pr(m)/dm$. Thus, one obtains

$$\frac{d \Pr(m)}{dm} = -P \Pr(m),$$

with solution

$$\Pr(m) = e^{-Pm}. \qquad (4\text{-}13)$$

Equation (4-13) gives the probability that any one site selection will be made on the range of sites beyond the m best (most accessible) ones. Conversely, the probability is $1 - e^{-Pm}$ that one of the m best sites is selected. Thus, if a total of N housing units are built, the expected number $n(m)$ of units on the m best sites is

$$n(m) = \text{(total number built) (probability that any one is}$$
$$\text{built on the } m \text{ best sites)}$$
$$= N(1 - e^{-Pm}).$$

Let

$$\rho(m) = \text{density of housing units as a function of } m$$

$$= \text{(number of housing units in the range } dm)/dm;$$

so

$$\rho(m) = \frac{dn(m)}{dm} = PNe^{-Pm}. \qquad (4\text{-}14)$$

The model so far does not guarantee that $\rho(m) < m$, and so the constants N and P must be chosen in such a way as to preclude overbuilding.

Suppose that vacant sites are available at a uniform spatial density of D units per square mile throughout the area. Suppose further that, for any radius r from the area center, the sites within r are viewed as more accessible than the sites outside. In this case, the number of sites within radius r is equal to the ordered site number m corresponding to radius r. The area enclosed by radius r is πr^2, and so $m(r) = D\pi r^2$. If this $m(r)$ is substituted into Eq. (4-14), one obtains

$$\rho(r) = \rho[m(r)] = PNe^{-PD\pi r^2}$$

or

$$\rho(r) = \rho(0)e^{-Cr^2}. \tag{4-15}$$

where $\rho(0) = PN$ = density at $r = 0$, and $C = PD\pi$, a constant. This function of housing density as a function of r in a uniform, circularly symmetric environment was first used in 1960 by Schneider [23] and by Sherratt [24].

(b) Time Dependence and Calibration

Let all the sites of the study area, built upon or vacant, be ordered according to decreasing accessibility, with labels $1, 2, \ldots, m, \ldots$. Let $v = v(m, t)$ be the number of sites, no less desirable than site m, still vacant at time t. Now the same argument, which led to Eq. (4-13), can be made to conclude that

$$\Pr(v) = e^{-Pv} = \text{probability that a site, selected at time } t, \text{ will be chosen to lie beyond the first } v \text{ most accessible sites.} \tag{4-16}$$

Equation (4-16) is the same as Eq. (4-13) except that the earlier m is replaced by $v = v(m, t)$.

Let the study area be divided into R zones and let v_i be the number of vacant sites in zone i at time t. Suppose that the zones are small enough so that they may be ordered according to their accessibility. Consider any one zone i. Let V_i be the total number of vacant sites at time t in *all* zones more accessible than the sites in zone i. Then, according to Eq. (4-16),

$$\Pr(V_i) = \exp[-PV_i] = \text{probability that a site selected at time } t \text{ will not be in the zones more accessible than zone } i,$$

and

$$\Pr(V_i + v_i) = \exp[-P(V_i + v_i)] = \text{probability that a site selected at time } t \text{ will not be either in the zones more accessible than zone } i \text{ or in zone } i.$$

Therefore,

$$\Pr(V_i) - \Pr(V_i + v_i) = \exp[-PV_i] - \exp[-P(V_i + v_i)] \tag{4-17}$$

is the probability that a site selected at time t will be in zone i.

The intervening opportunity model is used like the gravity model to predict the growth rate in each zone as a function of time. Let

$N(t)$ = the total number of housing units in the study area at time t. As before, this quantity is required as an input to the model.

$g(t)$ = $dN(t)/dt$ = study area growth rate at time t.

$n_i(t)$ = the number of housing units in zone i at time t. This is the quantity to be predicted. Note that

$$n_i(t) + v_i(t) = m_i,$$

where $v_i(t)$ is the number of vacant sites, and m_i is the total number of sites in zone i.

$g_i(t)$ = $dn_i(t)/dt$ = zone i growth rate at time t.

$N_i(t)$ = the number of housing units in all zones more accessible than zone i at time t. Note that

$$N_i(t) + V_i(t) = M_i,$$

where $V_i(t)$ is the number of vacant sites, and M_i is the total number of sites in the zones more accessible than zone i.

On the basis of Eq. (4-17),

$$g_i(t) = \frac{dn_i(t)}{dt} = g(t) \cdot \text{(probability that a site will be chosen in zone } i \text{ at time } t\text{)}$$

$$= g(t)\{\exp[-PV_i] - \exp[-P(V_i + v_i)]\}, \quad (4\text{-}18)$$

where $V_i = V_i(t) = M_i - N_i(t)$, and $v_i = v_i(t) = m_i - n_i(t)$.

The system of R differential equations (4-18), for $i = 1, \ldots, R$, is analogous to the gravity model equations (4-6). The most practical solution technique is to replace Eq. (4-18) by difference equations in the same manner as shown immediately after Eq. (4-6).

The model just developed has only one parameter P, to be obtained by calibration on known past growth patterns. One way is to seek the best least-squares fit by finding that value of P that minimizes

$$\sum_{i=1}^{R} [g_i(t) - g_{0i}(t)]^2,$$

where $g_{0i}(t)$ is the known growth rate, and $g_i(t)$ is the rate predicted by the model.

There is one calibration difficulty here which does not arise with the gravity model. Because the total number of sites is not bounded in the intervening opportunity model presented here, there will always be some small number of housing units assigned to sites less attractive than those in all explicitly enumerated zones. This problem can be handled by either (a) postulating an external world zone to include these embarrassing assignments or (b) normalizing the numbers obtained initially by scaling all upward in equal proportions so that

$$\sum_{i=1}^{R} g_i(t) \ = \ g(t).$$

Largely because there is only one parameter P to be fitted, the model in the present form cannot be expected to work very well. It has been suggested that P ought be a monotonically decreasing function of $N(t)$. Alternatively, perhaps P itself should be a function of the accessibility of the site to which it is applied.

Helly [13] exhibits further development of the time-dependent intervening opportunity model.

(c)   Cluster, Opportunity, and Trend Model (COT)

The intervening opportunity model is based only on the presumed desires of people to settle near their jobs, shopping opportunities, and other resources which characterize population centroids. Hartung [12] has developed a broader composite model, COT, which describes three behavioral aspects of the new household location process:

1.   The *cluster* component expresses the tendency of people to locate where others have already settled. It is assumed to be a fixed fraction of the number of total yearly new dwelling units for the entire study area. The fraction is obtained by calibration of the model to an appropriate data base. The cluster component is divided among the zones; so each zone receives an allocation proportional to the already existing total number of dwelling units in that zone.

2.   The *opportunity* component expresses the tendency of people to settle as near as possible to one or more centers of activity. This component also is a calibrated fixed fraction of the total yearly new dwelling units. It is allocated among the zones on the basis of a suitably calibrated intervening opportunity model.

3.   The *trend* component expresses the inertial tendency of development, whereby areas where much has been built recently are more likely to be developed further than are areas that have been stagnant. This component is the remaining fraction of total yearly new dwelling units not assigned to

the cluster or opportunity components. It is divided among the zones so that each zone receives an allocation proportional to the rate at which dwelling units have been increasing in that zone. Thus, the trend component is, in a sense, the derivative of the cluster component.

A partial reallocation is made whenever the cluster and trend components result in a zonal assignment of new dwelling units in excess of the presumed number of vacant sites in that zone. However, it is noted that "fully" built-up areas often experience zoning changes on a scale sufficient to maintain a nonempty inventory of vacant housing sites.

Hartung tested his model by calibrating it to observed 1955–1959 residential growth on Long Island, New York. The model was then used to predict the distribution of a phenomenal growth, 1960–1969, in all the townships of the study area. The predicted growths differed from those actually observed by a root-mean-square error of 22%. In contrast, a comparable pure intervening opportunity model forecast yielded a 34% root-mean-square error.

4-6   Land Market Models

The preceding models do not consider directly the economic aspects of the individual household's competition for desirable residential sites. Since this is a significant weakness, attempts have been made to develop cost or profit optimization models for location choice and consequent land development.

Industrial firms are more likely than private households to locate themselves solely on the basis of economic considerations. Hence early economic location analysis, pioneered by Weber (see Friedrich [7]), concerned itself only with industrial site selection. It was argued that a firm would locate so as to minimize its location-dependent costs. These costs are for delivery of raw materials, for utilities, for shipping of the finished product, and for the actual land used. In some cases, the supply and cost of labor must also be considered. The modeling process begins with the inscribing on maps of lines of equal inward shipping costs, of equal outward shipping costs, and of equal land rents. The minimum cost location can then be found by inspection, graphical analysis, or—in some cases—mathematical programming techniques. The approach has been elaborated by Isard [15], who included the economic interrelations within groups of firms operating at the same location.

Weberian analysis has been criticized for its reliance on the principle of cost minimization. Firms operate in a competitive environment, and hence it ought to be more realistic to assume that a location will be chosen to maximize profits rather than to minimize costs. Thus, a high rent or remote transport location may be chosen just because operation there is subject to less competition than at a minimum cost place. To overcome this objection, a quite complex "central-place theory," pioneered by Lösch [18], has received much attention. The central-place argument postulates genuine competition among firms, the maximum profit criterion for individual firms, and—for consumers—a minimum cost criterion for choosing among firms. Firms are assumed to dominate their immediate surroundings at the expense of firms located elsewhere. Where there are two areas, each dominated by firms in their central places, the boundary between the two is that physical line along which consumers are indifferent as to which center they patronize.

Economic optimization models have also been developed for the description of residential land development, despite the valid criticism that households generally have subtler optimization criteria than cost minimization or profit maximization. The models generally are based on the assumption that, given a household's income, family composition, and social status, one may deduce that household's available budget for its gross residential expenditures, which include land cost or rent, physical housing, and residence-based transportation.

Perhaps the simplest residential location model, at least conceptually, is by Muth [21], who argues that development proceeds toward an economic equilibrium. At equilibrium, the households will spend their entire gross residential budgets. Land prices will be such that a household's gross residential expenditure does not change with distance from the central business district. Let

$a(r)$ = "unit" price of housing, including land, as a function of distance r from the CBD,

$C(r)$ = individual household's consumption of housing, in the units used for $a(r)$, as a function of r, and

$R(r)$ = individual household's overall transportation costs, as a function of r.

The Muth equilibrium will be reached when

$$\frac{d}{dr}\left[a(r)C(r) + T(r)\right] = 0.$$

If the consumption of housing does not vary with r, then $C(r) = C$ and $C[da(r)/dr] = -[dT(r)/dr]$. The approach has been developed further by Alonso [1].

The Penn–Jersey model [14], formulated to forecast land use in the Philadelphia metropolitan area, is so far the most ambitious practical effort to thus describe the residential land market as based on trade-offs between land and transportation costs. Though not entirely successful, the original Penn–Jersey model was attractive enough to encourage further work [11, 22]. The chief difficulties encountered were in the calibration of the model to reproduce actual behavior of the location-dependent land prices. Some of the problems are:

1.   The land market is not an open one with perfect competition. Only some of the owners of development land are actually intent on maximizing their profits.

2.   Land values reflect subtle social considerations. The model cannot quantify these.

3.   One must find a practical way to aggregate the quite varied budget structures of different income groups.

Webber [27] offers a thorough review of location theory based on economic optimization principles.

4-7   Conclusion

This chapter has exhibited only a few of the best-known land-use models, all specialized to the residential site prediction problem. These, together with those not considered, are still quite imperfect, and there is much effort at improvement and the invention of new approaches. There are some very useful review articles, References [16, 17, 20], which together offer a fairly clear summary of the present state of the art.

The interested reader ought to go on to browse through *Geographic Perspectives on Urban Systems* [2], an almost monumental compendium on location theory and related subjects. Straud [26] offers a bibliography of almost 3000 works on urban geography, all published in the last 20 years.

PROBLEMS

Problems 1–3 consider the city of Miasma and its suburb Miasma Beach, as shown in Fig. 4-2, wherein the region is divided into zones by isochrones of equal travel time from the Miasma central business district. Table 4-2

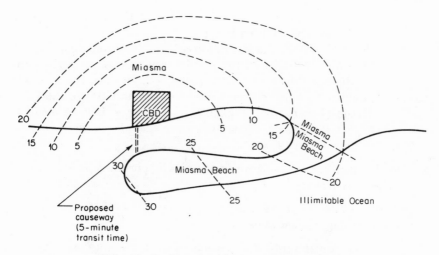

FIG. 4-2   Problem Area for Land-Use Forecasting

The dashed lines represent equal travel times, in minutes, from the Miasma central business district.

TABLE 4-2
Data for the Miasma Land-Use Forecasting Problem

Time from CBD, (minutes)	Miasma			Miasma Beach		
	Household sites	Households 1960	1970	Household sites	Households 1960	1970
0–5	1000	900	950	—		
5–10	4000	2000	2600	—		
10–15	10,000	2000	3000	—		
15–20	15,000	800	1200	2000	100	150
20–25	25,000	200	300	2000	20	40
25–30	40,000	50	100	2000	10	20
Total	95,000	5950	8150	6000	130	210

shows the number of households in each zone for both 1960 and 1970. It is estimated that the total 1980 population will be about 11,000 households for Miasma and Miasma Beach together.

1. Devise and apply a simple trend model to predict 1980 population for each zone.

2. (a) Calibrate a gravity model for predicting the zonal populations of Miasma and Miasma Beach.
   (b) Use the calibrated model to forecast the 1980 zonal populations.
   (c) Miasma is considering the possible construction of a causeway to Miasma Beach, as shown in Fig. 4-2. If built, the causeway would reduce travel time, from the Miasma CBD to the tip of Miasma Beach, from 30 minutes to 5 minutes. Use the model to predict 1980 zonal populations, given that the causeway is built and opened in 1975.

3. Do Problem 2, now using an intervening opportunity model instead of a gravity model.

4. Consider some specific residential area where there is in force minimum lot size zoning for new houses.

   (a) What are the ostensible reasons for such zoning? Are they rational? Does the zoning actually achieve the desired purposes?
   (b) It is observed in most places that, when there is minimum lot size zoning for houses, most houses are built on lots at or near to this minimum size. Is this true for your area? Would development differ significantly if the minimum lot size were different or if there were no zoning at all?

5. "While any one part of a metropolitan area can significantly affect its population, wealth, and social composition by zoning, it is unlikely that this can be done by a metropolitan area as a whole."

   Speculate on the truth of this assertion and on the advantages and disadvantages of localized zoning, coordinated metropolitan area zoning, and no zoning at all in shaping overall long-term development.

6. How might a gravity model be used to find the most profitable location for a new department store in a metropolitan area that already has a central business district and one or more non-CBD shopping centers?

REFERENCES

[1] Alonso, W., *Location and Land Use: Toward a General Theory of Land Rent.* Univ. of Hawaii, Honolulu, 1966.
[2] Berry, B. J. L., and Horton, F. E., *Geographic Perspectives on Urban Systems.* Prentice-Hall, Englewood Cliffs, New Jersey, 1970.
[3] *Calibrating and Testing a Gravity Model for Any Size Urban Area.* Bur. of Public Roads, Washington, D.C., 1965.

[4] Crecine, J. P., A time-oriented metropolitan model for spatial location. CRP Tech. Bull. No. 6. CONSAD Res. Corp., Pittsburgh, Pennsylvania, 1964.

[5] Cripps, E. L., and Foot, D. H. S., The urbanization effect of a third London airport. *Environment and Planning* 2, 153–192 (1970).

[6] Cripps, E. L., and Betty, M. J., Outline of research in the urban systems research unit. Urban Syst. Res. Unit, Univ. of Reading, Reading, England, 1969.

[7] Friedrich, C. J., *Alfred Weber's Theory of the Location of Industry*. Univ. of Chicago, Chicago, Illinois, 1929.

[8] Goldner, W., *Projective Land Use Model (PLUM)*. Bay Area Transportation Study Commission, San Francisco, California, 1968.

[9] Hamburg, J. R., and Sharkey, R. H., Land use forecast. Rep. 3.2.6.10. Chicago Area Transportation Study, Chicago, Illinois, 1961.

[10] Hanson, W. G., Land use forecasting for transportation planning. Highway Res. Board Bull. 253, pp. 145–151. Highway Res. Board, Washington, D.C., 1960.

[11] Harris, B., Basic assumptions for a simulation of the urban residential housing and land market. Inst. for Environmental Study, Univ. of Pennsylvania, Philadelphia, 1966.

[12] Hartung, J. V., Residential land use model with applications to Long Island. Ph.D. Dissertation, Polytech. Inst. of Brooklyn, New York, 1973.

[13] Helly, W., A time-dependent intervening opportunity land use model. *Socio-Economic Planning Sciences* 3, 65–73 (1969).

[14] Herbert, J., and Stevens, B. J., A model for the distribution of residential activities in urban areas. *Journal of Regional Science* 2, 21–36 (1960).

[15] Isard, W., *Location and Space-Economy*. MIT Press, Cambridge, Massachusetts, 1956.

[16] Kilbridge, M. D., O'Block, R. P., and Teplitz, P. V., A conceptual framework for urban planning models. *Management Science* 15, No. 6 (1969).

[17] King, L. J., *Models of Urban Land Use Development*. Battelle Memorial Inst., Pittsburgh, Pennsylvania, 1969.

[18] Lösch, A., *The Economics of Location*. Yale Univ. Press, New Haven, Connecticut, 1959.

[19] Lowry, I. S., A Model of Metropolis. No. RM 4035 RC. Rand Corp., Santa Monica, California, 1964.

[20] Lowry, I. S., Seven models of urban development: A structural comparison. Highway Res. Board Special Rept. 97, pp. 121–163. Highway Res. Board, Washington, D.C., 1968.

[21] Muth, R. F., The spatial structure of the housing market. *Papers and Proc. Regional Sci. Assoc., 1971*, 7, pp. 207–220.

[22] Schlager, K. J., A land use plan design model. *Journal of American Institute of Planners* 31, 103–111 (1965).

[23] Schneider, M., *Chicago Area Transportation Study—Vol. 2*, Chicago, Illinois, 1960.

[24] Sherrat, G. G., A model for general urban growth, *Management Sciences—Models and Techniques*, Vol. 2, pp. 147–159. Pergamon, Oxford, 1960.

[25] Stouffer, S. A., Intervening opportunities. *American Sociological Review* 5, No. 6 (1940).

[26] Strand, S., *Urban Geography, 1950–70: A Comprehensive Bibliography*. Bibliography Nos. 358–370. Council of Planning Librarians Exchange, Monticello, Illinois, 1973.

[27] Webber, M. J., *Impact of Uncertainty on Location*. MIT Press, Cambridge, Massachusetts, 1972.

Chapter *5*

Transportation Network

The ever more intense use of automobiles and trucks for transportation in urban areas has generated almost insatiable demands for space to accommodate these vehicles. This has led to well-known difficulties:

1.   Densely built areas do not have surplus land. Under pressure for an automotive way of life, they may partially demolish their existing structures to achieve a makeshift new balance. Even so, they tend to decay as activities move elsewhere.

2.   High-usage common carrier transit systems are caught in a squeeze whereby decreasing usage leads to poorer service which, in turn, encourages still greater automotive demands.

3.   Expressways and arterial roads form barriers across which it is difficult to maintain neighborhood cohesion. This factor may be even more important than noise or atmospheric pollution in causing neighboring land to lose its attractiveness for residential life.

Where an existing intensely developed town or neighborhood is viewed as an important asset to society, efforts are made to minimize the impact of automobiles. Public transit is encouraged; controls are devised to increase the efficiency of the limited road network; and—sometimes—serious efforts are made to inhibit automotive access. Such palliative measures do help, although so far they do not seem to have succeeded anywhere in achieving a satisfactory long-term equilibrium. There exists a most thoughtful study sponsored by the British government, known as the "Buchanan Report" [5], which addresses itself to the management of traffic in crowded urban centers. It uses a case study approach, applied to several problem areas, and it is highly recommended to the reader of this book.

Where an area has much vacant land, as in a sparsely developed suburb or a proposed "new town" site, there is much less of a problem in providing an adequate network for automobiles. However, even here one must anticipate a more crowded future and hence make frugal commitments of irreplaceable land.

In either case, effective planning requires means for predicting usage of the transportation network after it is augmented or changed, and after the population grows or shifts with the passage of time. The present chapter exhibits an integrated group of models, which predict road and transit usage as functions of where people live and work.

Again, as in the previous chapter, it should be pointed out that, because residential and work locations are based largely on access via the available transportation network, it is not really correct to decouple the transportation model from the land-use forecasting model. If really long-range forecasts are to be provided, it may be necessary to proceed iteratively by

(1)   predicting future land use, based on the present transportation system,

(2)   predicting the consequent travel patterns,

(3)   planning and postulating the construction of new transportation facilities, and

(4)   again going through steps (1) to (3)—repeatedly if it seems necessary.

5-1   Conceptual Framework for a Planning Model

Suppose that the city, or other study area, is divided into zones as discussed in Section 4-2. The basic transportation model package, described in this chapter, seeks to predict the traffic volume on each major street and transit segment in the study area, given

(a)   the number, composition, and resources of households, work places, commercial activities, schools, and other trip ends in each zone;

(b)   transportation system inventory which includes location, connections, capacity, and speed for each major segment of the road and transit network; and

(c)   the results of a travel survey, giving the volume of trips between most or all zone pairs, to be used for calibration.

The major components of the model package are

1. a *trip-generation model* for the synthesis of the number of trips, classified by purpose, originating in each zone of the study area;

2. a *trip-distribution model* for the apportionment of trips, originating in any one zone, among all possible destination zones;

3. a *modal-split model* for the apportionment of trips among possible transport modes; a two-way apportionment, to cars or public transit, is usually deemed to be sufficient;

4. an *assignment model* for the prediction of the routes followed by travelers using a given mode between any origin zone and any destination zone.

Whatever their forms, these models have to be calibrated and validated by application to present and/or past travel patterns, preferably in the area to be studied for the future. Calibration, based on present behavior, presents no problem where the models are to be used to plan immediate and modest change such as a road widening or secondary bridge. However, if the aim is to provide forecasts to a distant-time horizon or for a really major change in facilities, then the validity of the calibration procedures ought to be considered most carefully.

It is difficult to carry through the analysis for every type of trip. Fortunately, the main congestion problems arise in the rush hours when most trips are for the purpose of going to or from work. Hence it is customary to develop a detailed model only for work trips, either for an entire typical work day or for a characteristic rush hour.

In principle, the modeling process can be made fully time dependent so as to predict the moments at which all trips start, interact at en-route bottlenecks, and terminate at their destinations. Only if such time dependence is introduced can one do really accurate network assignment because the time taken by a traveler to traverse a network segment is dependent on the number of other travelers in his immediate vicinity.

In practice, there usually is not enough information to instrument meaningful time-dependent models, even on a probabilistic basis. Consequently, the models are developed in an essentially time-independent form, designed to exhibit the overall behavior for a single rush hour or a single day. These remarks are not to deny that there do exist small-scale applications, involving few zones and transport links, where it may indeed be possible to perform minute-by-minute time-dependent simulations.

5-2 Trip Generation

The aim of a trip-generation model is to predict the number of trips originating in each zone of the network. It usually is necessary to classify the trips by purpose because it is the rush hour travel to work that imposes the greatest strain on the transportation network. Generally, only the number of trips per day is forecast. Where volume variations within a day are required, it is assumed that the proportion of trips, made during any one time interval, will be the same proportion observed in the past. The *Highway Capacity Manual* [11] has summary information on how trips are distributed through the day.

Trips are made privately or for business. Private trips generally predominate, except perhaps at certain hours in the central business districts of very large cities. Thus it normally is sufficient to predict the number of trips originating at private residences. If these are predicted correctly, the remaining private trips, being mostly return journeys to homes, present little difficulty. The most useful predictor variables for residence-based trips appear to be population density, distance from the central business district, household income, mean household size, and car ownership.

It seems that population density and mean household income usually are sufficient for effective prediction of the mean number of trips per household. The other potentially useful predictor variables tend to add little to the forecast's accuracy.

For a model of present behavior, the number of households in any one zone and the consequent population density are observable quantities. For future forecasts, they are to be predicted by use of a suitable land-use model, as discussed in Chapter 4. A zone's mean household income is rather difficult to forecast for a distant-time horizon because substantial intraregional migration may occur in the interim. However, if the forecast is for a time only a few years hence, it may be reasonable to suppose that the ratio between a given zone's and the overall region's per household incomes will not change much from the present.

To deduce a valid relation between the predictor variables and the consequent number of home-based trips per household per day, one ought to conduct a travel survey in the particular study area of interest. Travel habits vary among cities, and results obtained in one place may be quite erroneous elsewhere. The survey results usually are organized by means of a regression analysis.

Example The Queens–Long Island Traffic Demand Study [19] used 1963–1964 travel surveys to deduce the following relation for the total number of trips to work in a 24-hour weekday:

$$t_i = L_i(0.815 + 0.0167I_i) \qquad \text{for} \quad I_i < \$7500 \text{ per year}$$

$$t_i = 0.94L_i \qquad \text{for} \quad I_i \geqq \$7500 \text{ per year}$$

Here t_i is the number of work trips generated in zone i during a 24-hour weekday; L_i is the number of workers living in the zone; and I_i is the median household income in the zone.

In this case, population density was not found sufficiently important for final inclusion in the regression equation. The mean number of workers per household was not reported. It was found that 90% of all trips to work occured between 7 and 10 A.M.

One may well question the long-term validity of a relation such as the one in the example. In particular, the number of trips per household tends to increase over the years. Of course, such an effect can be incorporated into the forecast, provided one has confidence in the argument therefor.

5-3   Trip Distribution

A trip-distribution model allocates the trips, originating in any one zone, among all the N possible destination zones of the study area (including the origin zone). The presently used methodologies for trip distribution seek to deduce the relative likelihood of any one destination by use of functions involving only the amount of activity at the destination and the cost, in time, of traveling to it.

The following notation will be used:

t_{Aij} = the presently observed actual number of trips, from zone i to zone j, during a specified time interval such as the average rush hour or the average 24-hour weekday. Then

$$t_{Ai} = \sum_{j=1}^{N} t_{Aij} = \text{presently observed total number}$$
$$\text{of trips originating in zone } i.$$

Note   A table of t_{Aij} is called a "trip table." It is needed to calibrate any trip-distribution model. Because it is difficult to obtain exact data, efforts often are made to synthesize approximately a complete trip table on the basis of small sample surveys among travelers.

t_{ij} = the corresponding number of trips from zone i to zone j, as predicted by the trip-distribution model. Then

$$t_i = \sum_{j=1}^{N} t_{ij} = \text{total number of trips originating in zone}$$
$$i \text{ today, as predicted by the model.}$$

The aim of calibration is to make the t_{ij}'s as nearly equal as possible to the t_{Aij}'s.

T_{ij} = the number of trips from zone i to zone j, as predicted by the trip-distribution model for a future time of interest. Then

$$T_i = \sum_{j=1}^{N} T_{ij} = \text{total number of trips originating in zone } i \text{ at some future time, as predicted by the model.}$$

T_{Ai} = estimate of the number of trips originating in zone i at the future time, obtained exogenously by means of a trip-generation analysis.

If the time interval is a 24-hour day, it is generally assumed that $t_{ij} = t_{ji}$, $t_{Aij} = t_{Aji}$, and $T_{ij} = T_{ji}$.

Among the models exhibited below, the gravity model is the one most widely used. The growth-factor models do not produce as good results, but are exhibited because of substantial use in the past. The intervening-opportunity model is of theoretical interest, but does not appear to have had serious application.

(a)   Growth-Factor Models

The idea is to distribute trips among zones on the basis of growth factors G_i, where

$$G_i = \left(\frac{T_{Ai}}{t_{Ai}}\right) = \frac{\text{predicted future trips originating in zone } i}{\text{observed present trips originating in zone } i}.$$

The simplest approach is the "average-growth-factor" model, wherein the growth in trips, from zone i to zone j, is set to be proportional to the average of the two zonal growths. Thus,

$$\left(\frac{T_{ij}}{t_{Aij}}\right) = K_1 \left[\frac{G_i + G_j}{2}\right].$$

The constant of proportionality K_1 must be chosen so that $\sum_{j=1}^{N} T_{ij} = T_{Ai}$, where T_{Ai} is the total number of trips generated by zone i. If this is done, one finds

$$T_{ij} = T_{Ai}[t_{Aij}(G_i + G_j)/\sum_{n=1}^{N} t_{Ain}(G_i + G_n)]. \qquad (5\text{-}1)$$

Another growth-factor formulation, known as the Fratar model [9], assumes that the growth in trips, from i to j, is proportional to the product of the growths in the two zones; so

$$(T_{ij}/t_{Aij}) = K_2[G_i G_j].$$

K_2 also must be chosen so that the sum of all trips from zone i adds up to T_{Ai}. If this is done, one finds

$$T_{ij} = T_{Ai}[t_{Aij}G_j / \sum_{n=1}^{N} t_{Ain}G_n].$$ (5-2)

There is evidence [4] that the average-growth-factor and the Fratar models are about equally accurate.

Growth-factor models are inherently limited in that they fail to incorporate the effects of changes in the transportation system. For example, the travel time between two riverside zones, originally connected by a slow ferry, would be much reduced by the completion of a direct bridge. Obviously, the growth-factor models will not forecast the consequent increase in the number of trips between these zones.

(b) The Gravity Model

The growth-factor approach does not consider the effects of travel time or costs on the allocation of trips among destinations. Hence it is useless for assessing the effects of transportation system changes, which substantially affect travel times. The gravity model, a construct closely analogous to the identically named land-use formulation, overcomes this difficulty [22].

It is assumed that the number of trips between two zones is proportional to the total number of trips emanating from the origin zone i, the total number of trips terminating at the destination zone j, and a friction factor F_{ij} which represents the "cost," usually taken as a function of travel time, between the two zones:

$$T_{ij} = T_{Ai}[A_j F_{ij} / \sum_{k=1}^{N} A_k F_{ik}].$$ (5-3)

Here A_j is either the number of trips terminating in zone j or, if this is not known, a measure of that number. For example, if work trips are to be distributed, then A_j can be the number of jobs in zone j. The sum in the denominator ensures that $\sum_{j=1}^{N} T_{ij} = T_i$.

This model must be calibrated by finding an appropriate set of values for the friction factors F_{ij}. It is customary to assume that F_{ij} is a function *only* of the travel time between zones i and j. Calibration is performed by applying the model to the presently observed trip table, for which the t_{ij}'s are known; so the corresponding F_{ij}'s can be calculated in the same way as in Section 4-4(b). The F_{ij}'s are then plotted against the corresponding travel times, and a single-valued function F of travel time is fitted to the data. If Eq. (5-3), incorporating this composite function, reproduces the calibration distribution well, then it is assumed that the model has utility. It is hoped that the travelers' discrimination among differing travel times will not change in the future.

Sometimes it helps to include one or more correction factors in the above described basic friction function. For example, costly tolls or subtle psychological factors may make a river a greater barrier to travel than can be explained on the basis of travel times alone. In such a case, one can introduce an additional parameter to increase F for all trips crossing the barrier.

If it is deemed necessary that the number of trips terminating in a zone j, $\sum_{i=1}^{N} T_{ij}$, be equal to the number T_j originating in that zone, iterative adjustments of the results will be required.

(c) *The Intervening-Opportunity Model*

This model is almost identical to the intervening-opportunity formalism for land-use forecasting, Section 4-5. In the land-use formulation, it was argued that the choice of a site in zone j has probability

$$\exp(-pV_j) - \exp[-p(V_j + v_j)],$$

where V_j is the number of vacant sites more accessible than the sites in zone j, v_j is the number of vacant sites in zone j, and p is a parameter to be fitted to observed behavior.

For trip distribution, it is argued that a trip, originating in zone i, will terminate in zone j with probability

$$\exp(-pM_{ij}) - \exp[-p(M_{ij} + m_j)],$$

where M_{ij} is the number of trip ends (or trip attractions) more accessible to zone i than are the trip ends in zone j, and m_j is the number of trip ends in zone j. On this basis,

$$T_{ij} = T_i\{\exp(-pM_{ij}) - \exp[-p(M_{ij} + m_j)]\}. \qquad (5\text{-}4)$$

The parameter p must be calibrated on the basis of a suitable observed trip table. It may well be made a function of travel time or other explicative variables.

The intervening-opportunity model was used by the Chicago Area Transportation Study [6]. However, it is not held in great esteem because the ordering of zones and calibration present serious difficulties in practice. A critique is given by Whitaker and Kent [24].

(d) Wilson's Entropy Formulation

Wilson [25] has devised a statistical basis for the gravity and inter-vening-opportunity models. His formulation can be used to generate further models and thus may well be suitable as a basis for new theoretical work. Wilson's approach will be illustrated here by a derivation of a gravity-type model.

The predicted trip distribution will be a trip table $\{T_{ij}\}$, which must satisfy the constraints

$$\sum_{j=1}^{N} T_{ij} = O_i, \qquad \sum_{i=1}^{N} T_{ij} = D_j, \qquad \sum_{i=1}^{N} \sum_{j=1}^{N} T_{ij} = T. \tag{5-5}$$

Here, O_i (previously labeled T_i) is the number of trips originating in zone i; D_j is the number terminating in j; and T is the total number of trips.

A further constraint is postulated to fix a total "cost" C for all trips:

$$\sum_{i=1}^{N} \sum_{j=1}^{N} T_{ij} c_{ij} = C. \tag{5-6}$$

The generalized cost c_{ij}, for a trip between zones i and j, need not be elapsed time alone. It may well be some composite function of time, distance, and money cost.

The trip table $\{T_{ij}\}$ is viewed as a set of random variables. Wilson's basic assumption is that any particular set of $\{T_{ij}\}$ will actually occur with a probability which is proportional to the number of states of the system that yield the particular set of values. Let $w(T_{ij})$ be the number of distinct arrangements of individual trips that result in a particular trip table $\{T_{ij}\}$. Then

$$w(T_{ij}) = T! / \prod_{i=1}^{N} \prod_{j=1}^{N} T_{ij}!. \tag{5-7}$$

The denominator arises because there is no meaningful difference among arrangements within any one trip bundle T_{ij}.

Example Suppose there are $N = 3$ zones and that one particular distribution T_{ij} of $T = 6$ trips is given by

$$\{T_{ij}\} = \begin{bmatrix} 0 & 2 & 1 \\ 1 & 0 & 0 \\ 2 & 0 & 0 \end{bmatrix}.$$

Here the jth element of the ith row is T_{ij}; thus $T_{12} = 2$. The number of distinct arrangements of $T = 6$ trips that result in the given $\{T_{ij}\}$ is

$$w(T_{ij}) = 6!/2!2!1!1! = 720/4 = 180.$$

The procedure now is to find that one trip table $\{T_{ij}\}$ that maximizes the function $w(T_{ij})$, subject to the constraints (5-5) and (5-6). By Wilson's basic assumption, this $\{T_{ij}\}$ is the most likely distribution and therefore appropriate for one's forecast.

It is convenient to maximize $\log w(T_{ij})$, rather than $w(T_{ij})$, because then Stirling's approximation can be used:

$$\log N! \simeq N \log N - N, \qquad \text{so} \qquad \frac{\partial \log N!}{\partial N} \simeq \log N.$$

Using Lagrange multipliers, the values of T_{ij} that maximize $w(T_{ij})$, subject to Eqs. (5-5) and (5-6), are found by maximizing

$$M = \log w(T_{ij}) + \sum_{i=1}^{N} \lambda_i^{(1)}(O_i - \sum_{j=1}^{N} T_{ij})$$

$$+ \sum_{j=1}^{N} \lambda_j^{(2)}(D_j - \sum_{i=1}^{N} T_{ij}) + \beta(C - \sum_{i=1}^{N}\sum_{j=1}^{N} T_{ij}c_{ij}),$$

where $\lambda_i^{(1)}$, $\lambda_j^{(2)}$, and β are the Lagrangian multipliers. The T_{ij}'s that maximize M are the solutions of $\partial M/\partial T_{ij} = 0$ and the constraint equations (5-5) and (5-6). One finds

$$\frac{\partial M}{\partial T_{ij}} = -\log T_{ij} - \lambda_i^{(1)} - \lambda_j^{(2)} - \beta c_{ij} = 0,$$

with solution

$$T_{ij} = \exp(-\lambda_i^{(1)} - \lambda_j^{(2)} - \beta c_{ij}).$$

If one defines

$$A_i = \exp(-\lambda_i^{(1)})/O_i \qquad \text{and} \qquad B_j = \exp(-\lambda_j^{(2)})/D_j,$$

one obtains

$$T_{ij} = A_i B_j O_i D_j \exp(-\beta c_{ij}), \qquad (5\text{-}8)$$

where

$$A_i = [\sum_{j=1}^{N} B_j D_j \exp(-\beta c_{ij})]^{-1} \qquad \text{and} \qquad B_j = [\sum_{i=1}^{N} A_i O_i \exp(-\beta c_{ij})]^{-1}.$$

The most probable distribution of trips, as given by Eq. (5-8), is essentially the gravity-model formulation, wherein T_{ij} is proportional to the number of trip origins in i and the number of destinations in j. A_i, B_j, and β are there to ensure that the constraints are met. The exponential term in Eq. (5-8) need not be evaluated explicitly unless a specific cost is to be used in constraint (5-6).

Wilson's formulation is known as an "entropy" model because of a close parallel to the definition and use of the entropy function in thermodynamics. Potts and Oliver [17] offer a further, more general analysis of this approach.

5-4 Modal Split

Where facilities for private automobile travel are overloaded or where there is some concern for the travel needs of the old, the young, or the poor, there may be efforts to improve public transit. Characteristically, such efforts usually appear in the form of proposals to build or augment transit for commuters in urban areas. In assessing the utility of these proposals, it is useful to estimate the patronage that would be diverted to transit as a result of their implementation. Further, any forecast, in an environment where transit exists, ought to allocate trips properly among modes so that points of congestion are pinpointed correctly.

When travelers are in a position to choose among two or more travel modes, the individual makes his choice on the bases of relative costs, travel times, convenience, comfort, status values, and possibly still other considerations. His conclusions will certainly be affected by his age, by whether or not he owns a car, and by his financial resources. A modal-split model seeks to use some of these considerations, viewed as predictor variables, to forecast the proportion of travelers who choose each available mode. The significant models to date have used a statistical approach, known as discriminant analysis, for which a variety of theoretical formulations can be found in Reference [23]. Recent models by Stopher [20], Bevis [3], and Pratt [18] seem to be particularly effective, and the following presentation is a sort of amalgam of these.

The viewpoint taken is that of the individual traveler who evaluates the overall disutility (i.e., generalized cost) to himself of each competing travel mode. He chooses that mode which, to him, appears to have the minimum disutility. Assume that:

1. Commuters have a choice between two travel modes, A and B.

2. The disutility C of any trip, by either mode, is assumed to be a function of r predictor variables q_i, $i = 1, 2, \ldots, r$. We assume here that the function is linear; so

$$C = \sum_{i=1}^{r} a_i q_i,$$

where the a_i's are coefficients to be found by calibrating the model to existing data.

3. Each traveler acts as though he views the disutility difference, between modes A and B, to be

$$\Delta C = C^{\mathrm{A}} - C^{\mathrm{B}} = \sum_{i=1}^{r} a_i(q_i{}^{\mathrm{A}} - q_i{}^{\mathrm{B}}),$$

where the q_i's are those that apply to the two mode choices for his trip.

4. If $\Delta C \leq 0$, the traveler chooses mode A. If $\Delta C > 0$, the traveler chooses mode B.

5. The aim of the modal-split model is to provide a statistical discriminant function $F = F(\Delta C)$ such that $F(\Delta C)$ = proportion of travelers who will choose mode B when the "objective" disutility difference, between modes A and B, is $\Delta C = C^{\mathrm{A}} - C^{\mathrm{B}}$. Since individuals' evaluation of ΔC may vary, the "objective" value usually is defined as the mean of the individuals' values.

The model structure specified by these assumptions may be developed at various levels of sophistication. We shall present two levels; the second is the more difficult one to calibrate. Before doing so, we illustrate the formulation of cost functions by exhibiting two used in actual studies.

Helly [10]: For the mode choice between taxi and airport limousine for business travelers between Manhattan and New York airports, the predictor variables were

q_1 = total time cost in hours

q_2 = total money cost in dollars.

Calibration showed that, approximately, 1 hour was equivalent to \$10, so $C \cong q_1 + 0.1q_2$.

Pratt [18]: For a mode choice between auto and transit for commuters in Minneapolis–St. Paul, the predictor variables were

q_1 = driving or running cost in hours,

q_2 = excess time (parking, walking, waiting) in hours,

q_3 = total money cost in dollars.

Calibration showed that if $a_1 = 1$, then $a_2 = 2.5$, and $a_3 = (0.25 \, \$_w)^{-1}$, where $\$_w$ is the commuter's wage in dollars per hour. Thus,

$$C \cong q_1 + 2.5q_2 + (q_3/0.25 \, \$_w).$$

(a) Linear Discriminant Function

One assumes that $F(\Delta C)$ is a symmetric linear function of ΔC, as shown in Fig. 5-1,

$$F(\Delta C) = \begin{cases} 0, & \text{if} \quad \Delta C < -(1/2b) \\ \tfrac{1}{2} + b \, \Delta C, & \text{if} \quad -(1/2b) \leqq \Delta C \leqq (1/2b). \\ 1, & \text{if} \quad \Delta C > (1/2b) \end{cases} \qquad (5\text{-}9)$$

Here b is a constant to be determined. This definition of $F(\Delta C)$ is the only linear formulation that ensures that the probability of either mode is $\frac{1}{2}$ when $\Delta C = 0$.

To calibrate this discriminant function, one requires data for a number N of travelers. Each traveler is asked to consider his regular trip and to

(a)   estimate the predictor variables for both travel modes;
(b)   tell which mode he chooses to use.

The data thus obtained consist of

$q_{ij}{}^A$, $q_{ij}{}^B$ = predictor variable i, estimated for modes A and B by traveler j.

$Y_j = 0$ if traveler j chooses mode A.
$Y_j = 1$ if traveler j chooses mode B.

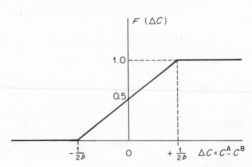

FIG. 5-1   Linear Discriminant Approximation for Modal Split

$F(\Delta C)$ is the proportion of travelers who choose mode B when the disutility difference between modes A and B is $\Delta C = C^A - C^B$.

Then, for traveler j, the central linear part of Eqs. (5-9) becomes

$$F(\Delta C_j) = \tfrac{1}{2} + b \, \Delta C_j = \tfrac{1}{2} + \sum_{i=1}^{r} e_i(q_{ij}{}^{A} - q_{ij}{}^{B}),$$

where $e_i = ba_i$.

It is desired that $F(\Delta C) \to 1$ if mode B is chosen by most people and that $F(\Delta C) \to 0$ if mode A is generally chosen. Since $Y_j = 1$ when B is chosen and $Y_j = 0$ when A is chosen, it is reasonable to suppose that the parameters e_i ought to be found by minimizing

$$G = \sum_{j=1}^{N} [F(\Delta C_j) - Y_j]^2$$

$$= \sum_{j=1}^{N} [\tfrac{1}{2} + \sum_{i=1}^{r} e_i(q_{ij}{}^{A} - q_{ij}{}^{B}) - Y_j]^2. \qquad (5\text{-}10)$$

A rigorous justification of Eq. (5-10) can be found in Reference [13].

To minimize G, one solves the set of N linear algebraic equations $\partial G/\partial e_i = 0$, $i = 1, 2, \ldots, N$, for the appropriate values of e_i.

(b) Normal Discriminant Function

One assumes that $F(\Delta C)$ is the cumulative normal distribution:

$$F(\Delta C) = \frac{1}{(2\pi)^{1/2}\sigma_{\Delta C}} \int_{-\infty}^{\Delta C} \exp\left[-\frac{1}{2}\left(\frac{x - \overline{\Delta C}}{\sigma_{\Delta C}}\right)^2\right] dx. \qquad (5\text{-}11)$$

The reasoning for this function is as follows: The individual traveler does not estimate the disutility difference ΔC between the two modes with precision. One supposes that his evaluation is a value drawn from an error distribution about the "true" disutility difference $\overline{\Delta C}$. The normal distribution, Eq. (5-11), is assumed to be this error distribution. $\sigma_{\Delta C}{}^2$ is the variance among travelers in evaluating the same disutility difference.

In principle, Eq. (5-11) can be calibrated by the same procedure as was used for the linear form (5-9). However, when derivatives, with respect to the predictor variables, are set equal to zero, one is faced with a formidable set of nonlinear equations. Hence the problem will not be followed further here; further analysis can be found in the literature [1, 23].

5-5   Assignment

Assignment is the prediction of the route, or routes, taken by travelers between origin and destination zones of the network. Usually one postulates that each traveler takes the fastest or, at least, one of the two or three fastest available routes. The following description addresses itself to the assignment of automobile trips to the street and highway network. Transit assignment is done in the same manner, applied to the appropriate network of actual transit services.

(a)   Coding the Network

A *graph* is a mathematical description of the network's spatial structure. The network graph consists of *links*, sometimes called branches, and *nodes*. A link represents a small physical segment of the network. We shall require that all links be *directed*, meaning that traffic can traverse each only in one specified direction. Each link originates at one node and terminates at another. Nodes are used (a) to join links together and (b) to represent *sources* (i.e., origins) or *sinks* (i.e., destinations) of traffic.

Let the network nodes be labeled $1, 2, \ldots, N$. Let there be *at most* one directed link (i, j) from node i to node j. If there is two-way traffic between i and j, one uses two links, (i, j) and (j, i). In this way, it is possible to describe completely the structure of the network by a listing of its links. For example, the graph of Fig. 5-2 is described by $[(1, 2), (2, 3), (2, 5), (3, 4), (4, 5), (5, 2), (5, 6), (6, 3)]$. In such a graph, a *chain* from node i to node j is any set of connected links that provides a route from i to j. In the figure, $[(1, 2), (2, 5), (5, 6)]$ is a chain from node 1 to node 6. No chain is possible from 6 to 1 because no link terminates at node 1. A chain that terminates at its origin node is called a *cycle*.

Let a *tree* be a group of chains from one origin node to one or more destination nodes, set up in such a way that

(1)   there is only one chain from the origin to any destination, and
(2)   there is no cycle in the tree.

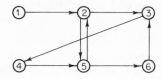

FIG. 5-2   The Graph of a Network

The above definitions are sufficient for the present discussion. However, a far more extensive terminology has been developed (see Ford and Fulkerson [8]).

Associated with each link (i, j), there is a link "cost" c_{ij}, usually taken to be the time needed by the traveler to traverse the link. Depending on the sophistication of one's model, c_{ij} may be viewed as constant or can be made a function which increases with the total volume of traffic actually assigned to use the link.

Each vehicle is assumed to enter or leave the network at specified origin or destination nodes. The basic assignment model works on the premise that the vehicle will travel along the chain, between origin and destination, that minimizes the sum of the link costs for its trip. An assignment of the network traffic is the application of this principle to all trips; so one may obtain the number of trips using each link.

The accuracy of assignment depends critically on the accuracy with which origin–destination chain costs, obtained from the network graph, reproduce actual travel times. Hence great care must be exercised in graphing the real network. Simplification is inevitable; even for small cities it is not practical to reproduce every local access street and intersection. One, therefore, seeks to choose the more significant arterial streets and highways.

Figure 5-3 shows a fairly obvious way to graph a street grid. The nodes are placed at intersections, and the links describe the street segments between intersections. For each zone, an additional node is added, with zero cost links connecting it to the principal intersection of the zone. This additional node is used as the source for trips originating in the zone. It is also used as the sink for trips terminating there. While the approach of

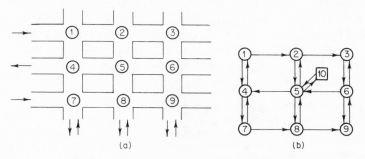

FIG. 5-3 Network Graph—Nodes at Intersections

(a) Part of street network—arrows show directions of permitted traffic flow; nodes are placed at intersections. (b) Graph of the network—Node 10 is added to represent the zone's trip ends; (5, 10) and (0, 5) are zero-cost links.

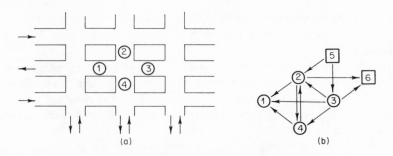

FIG. 5-4   Network graph—Node between Intersections

(a) Part of street network—nodes are placed between intersections; (b) graph of the central intersection area—nodes 5 and 6 are added to represent the zone's trip ends. $(2, 6)$, $(4, 6)$, $(5, 2)$, and $(5, 4)$ are zero cost links.

Fig. 5-3 can work reasonably well, a more sophisticated graph may be preferable. Consider:

1.   Delays often are more significant at the intersections than in between. Since travel times are associated with the links, it is more appropriate to have the links pass through intersections and to place the nodes at mid-block points.

2.   Turns at intersections contribute substantially to travel times. If nodes are placed at the intersections, then it is rather difficult to include time penalties for making turns. Further, some turns may be prohibited. Again, placing nodes at mid-block points will overcome this problem.

3.   If all trips ending in a zone are injected and absorbed at one intersection node, there may be unrealistic congestion in the neighborhood of that node. Hence, it may be wise to have zonal trip ends occur at more than one node. If this is done, the single-zone terminal node should be replaced by two nodes, one for the origin and the other for the destination. If only one terminal node is used, and connected to the graph by zero-cost links, then that node can be used improperly for zero cost shortcuts from one network node to another.

Figure 5-4 shows a graph, which applies these principles to the central intersection of the Fig. 5-3 network.

(b)   All-or-Nothing Assignment with Fixed Link Costs

A very simple model is based on the following two approximations:

1.   *All-or-nothing assignment*   All traffic, from one zone to another, is

routed along the one "shortest" (minimum time cost) route between the origin node and the destination node.

2.   *Fixed link costs*   The time cost c_{ij} for traversing any link (i, j) is estimated in advance of the assignment. c_{ij} is kept constant regardless of how much traffic is assigned to (i, j).

The all-or-nothing assumption is reasonable when one route is substantially faster than all others for a given origin–destination pair. It may cause major errors when two or more routes have nearly equal travel times. The fixed-link-cost assumption is reasonable if the originally chosen link travel times result in predicted link travel volumes consistent with these times. However, if a link travel time is made too small, the link may be assigned more traffic than its real-life counterpart could possibly handle.

Given a trip table, resulting from a trip-distribution analysis, together with a graph of the network and estimated time costs for all links, it only remains to find the minimum-cost routes for the origin–destination pairs that occur in the trip table. The traffic can then be assigned to these minimum-cost routes. One very simple algorithm [12], easily programmed for a digital computer, obtains a tree of minimum-cost routes from any one node to all other nodes of the network. The procedure is as follows:

1.   Start building the tree by including within it only the origin node.

2.   Identify the one as yet unconnected node that is nearest to the origin node. This *must be* one of the nodes reachable *via a single link* from the tree already developed at this stage. If two or more nodes are equally close, choose any one of them. The chosen node and the link connecting it to the tree are added to the tree.

3.   Repeat step 2 until all required nodes have been added to the tree.

This algorithm is illustrated on the graph of Fig. 5-5(a), which is the same as the one in Fig. 5-2, now redrawn with a link cost c_{ij} shown next to each link (i, j). Let node 1 be the origin node. Let $C_t(n)$ be the cost of the

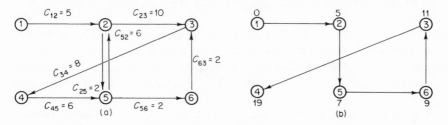

FIG. 5-5   Illustration of the Minimum-Cost Tree Algorithm

(a) A network graph with link costs; (b) minimum-cost tree from node 1.

TABLE 5-1
Illustration of the Minimum-Cost Tree Algorithm

Step number	Nodes within one link of tree	Cost from origin to node	Closest node n added to tree	$C_t(n)$	Link added to tree
1		Start with node 1	1	0	—
2	2	5	2	5	(1, 2)
3	3	$C_t(2) + 10 = 15$	5	7	(2, 5)
	5	$C_t(2) + 2 = 7$			
4	3	$C_t(2) + 10 = 15$	6	9	(5, 6)
	6	$C_t(5) + 2 = 9$			
5	3	$C_t(2) + 10 = 15$, or	3	11	(6, 3)
		$C_t(6) + 2 = 11$			
6	4	$C_t(3) + 8 = 19$	4	19	(3, 4)

cheapest route (chain) from the origin node to node n. Table 5-1 shows how $C_t(n)$ is calculated for all n. The resultant minimum-cost tree is shown in Fig. 5-5(b).

Other algorithms for building minimum-cost trees, together with FORTRAN programs for their use, are given by Martin [15]. The United States Department of Transportation has available an IBM 7094 computer program package for large-scale assignments [21]. A revision for the IBM 360 series computers is in prospect.

(c)   *Variable Link Costs: Capacity Constraint*

In the real world, the travel time or cost of a link is a function of the volume of traffic on that link. Formally, the cost c_{ij} of (i, j) really should be $c_{ij} = c_{ij}(n_{ij})$, where n_{ij} is the number of vehicles on (i, j). This cost increases rapidly when the link capacity is approached; hence the name "capacity constraint."

A simple, somewhat awkward way to assign traffic with capacity constraint is to make iterative assignments on a fixed-link-cost basis. For each new iteration, the link costs are recomputed, using the assigned link traffic obtained in the previous iteration. To get reasonably rapid convergence and to avoid oscillations among incorrect assignments, some ingenuity is required in choosing the extent to which the costs are adjusted between iterations.

There is much recent interest in improving the methodology of capacity-constrained assignment. Especially notable is the work of Dafermos [7], which is discussed and expanded on by Potts and Oliver [17].

(d)   Multiple Routes and Diversion Assignment

When two or more routes between two zones offer near minimal costs to the travelers, it is not correct to assume that all traffic goes only on the cheapest one. Because there is not as yet a really satisfactory method for multiple-route assignment, most workers have ignored this consideration.

Some use has been made of a rather irrational approach. Several all-or-nothing assignments are averaged, each one using a somewhat different set of link costs. A variant of this procedure is to assign the traffic a little at a time, on an all-or-nothing basis, and to recompute travel times after each traffic increment is added [14].

When traffic between two zones uses two or more definitely known routes, with known costs, the modal-split methodology, Section 5-4, can be used. In this case, each of the routes can be viewed as one mode of travel between origin node and destination node. The modal-split approach to multiple-route assignment is called "diversion assignment." It is especially useful in estimating the traffic that is likely to be diverted onto a proposed new link in the network, such as a bridge.

5-6   Conclusion

The overall approach shown here has been used for predicting future travel patterns for many major cities, including Baltimore [2], Chicago [6], and Pittsburgh [16]. Results have been useful, although no one claims that great accuracy is assured. There still is much scope for research to improve the models.

Special mention ought to be made of the book *Flows in Transportation Networks* by Potts and Oliver [17], wherein models for trip distribution and assignment are developed in a very thorough and sophisticated manner. New research results generally appear in the journals *Transportation Research* and *Transportation Science* and in the publications of the Highway Research Board.

This chapter has been devoted to the descriptive modeling of transportation networks on a macroscopic scale. When one is concerned with smaller scale phenomena, such as congestion at bottlenecks, one usually must resort to stochastic modeling, as discussed in the next chapter. Neither chapter deals seriously with the problems of *controlling* the traffic so as to achieve optimum utilization of the available facilities. These problems are numerous and important, and so the quite sophisticated discipline of traffic engineering has evolved to cope with them. The *Highway Capacity Manual* [11] is a useful introduction and a compendium of established methods.

PROBLEMS

1. (a) Use the average growth-factor model to predict T_{ij}, for $i = 1, 2, 3$, given

i	T_{Ai}	t_{Ai1}	t_{Ai2}	t_{Ai3}
1	1000	0	300	200
2	2000	1000	0	1000
3	3000	700	300	0

(*Answer:* $T_{12} = 473$, etc.)

   (b) Repeat part (a), now using the Fratar model.

Answer: $T_{12} = 333$, etc.)

   (c) Suppose that, in part (a), it is required that $T_{ij} \cong T_{ji}$. Devise a method for adjusting the results that satisfies this requirement, yet keeps, as far as possible, the relative magnitudes of the initially calibrated T_{ij}'s.

2. Let there be two residential zones, 1 and 2, and two industrial zones, 3 and 4. It is predicted that in 1980 there will be 1000 commuters from zone 1 to zones 3 and 4, and 3000 commuters from zone 2 to zones 3 and 4. Each of the zones 3 and 4 is expected to employ 2000 of the workers originating in zones 1 and 2. Suppose that a gravity model has been calibrated, on 1970 data, to show $F_{13} = 2$, $F_{14} = 5$, $F_{23} = 3$, and $F_{24} = 4$.

   (a) Use the gravity model to estimate the distribution of work trips from zones 1 and 2.

(*Answer:* $T_{13} = 285$, etc.)

(b) The results of part (a) are inconsistent with the predicted employment levels in zones 3 and 4. Devise a method for adjusting the friction factors, in as uniform a way as possible, so that approximate consistency is obtained.

3. Suppose that $r = 2$ predictor variables are to be used in the linear modal-split model. Show that the values of e_1 and e_2, which minimize Eq. (5-10), are found by solving the following pair of linear algebraic equations:

$$e_1 \sum_{j=1}^{N} (\Delta q_{1j})^2 + e_2 \sum_{j=1}^{N} \Delta q_{1j} \, \Delta q_{2j} = \sum_{j=1}^{N} (Y_j - \tfrac{1}{2}) \, \Delta q_{1j},$$

$$e_1 \sum_{j=1}^{N} \Delta q_{1j} \, \Delta q_{2j} + e_2 \sum_{j=1}^{N} (\Delta q_{2j})^2 = \sum_{j=1}^{N} (Y_j - \tfrac{1}{2}) \, \Delta q_{2j},$$

where $\Delta q_{ij} = q_{ij}^A - q_{ij}^B$ for $i = 1, 2$.

4. A sample of size $N = 8$ of New York City car owners were asked to estimate travel times and travel costs for their trips to work (a) using their cars, and (b) using the subway system. They also were asked which mode they used. The survey results:

Car owner number	Travel time (minutes)		Travel cost ($)		Mode chosen
	Car	Subway	Car	Subway	
1	10	25	1.00	0.35	car
2	15	25	3.00	0.35	subway
3	30	30	2.50	0.35	subway
4	20	30	4.00	0.35	subway
5	20	15	2.00	0.35	subway
6	20	40	1.50	0.35	car
7	30	60	2.00	0.70	car
8	20	40	1.00	0.35	car

Use these data and the result of Problem 3 to calibrate the linear modal-split model of Eqs. (5-9) and (5-10).

5. Figure 5-6 shows the graph of a network with fixed travel times along its links. All links can be traversed in both directions. Nodes 1, 3, and 5 are zonal origin–destination points.

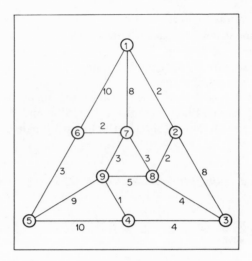

FIG. 5-6 Network Graph for Problem 5

(a) Find minimum-travel-time trees from nodes 1, 3, and 5 to the network.

(b) Given $T_{13} = T_{31} = 300$, $T_{15} = T_{51} = 200$, and $T_{35} = T_{53} = 400$, assign the traffic to the network.

(c) If a unit reduction in travel time could be made on just one link, which link should be chosen? How great a reduction of travel time could be made on that link before the original network assignment becomes invalid?

6. If a two-way street is converted to one-way operation and if the traffic volume remains the same as before, the average speed of vehicles will increase. Alternatively, the street will be able to handle more vehicles than before at the same average speed. However, there is a penalty in that, when a street network is converted to one-way operation, the average trip length is increased. Suppose that the streets of a central business district, consisting of a square grid of $N \times N$ blocks, is to be converted from two-way to one-way operation.

(a) For two-way operation, estimate the average trip length, in blocks, for trips that both start and terminate within the district. Estimate also the average length, of the CBD portion of the trip, for trips that have either origin or destination outside the CBD.

(b) Repeat part (a) for one-way street operation.

(c)   Given that a fraction f_1 of the trips has both origin and destination within the district, f_2 has either origin or destination within the district, and $(1 - f_1 - f_2)$ passes through without stopping, what is the fractional increase in apparent traffic volume which will result from one-way operation?

(d)   Formulate a conclusion about the circumstances under which one-way streets may not improve traffic performance.

REFERENCES

[1]   Anderson, T. W., *Introduction to Multivariate Statistics*. Wiley, New York, 1947.

[2]   *Baltimore Metropolitan Area Transportation Study*, Wilbur Smith & Assoc., New Haven, Connecticut, 1964.

[3]   Bevis, H. W., A probabilistic model for highway traffic assignment. *Annu. Meeting Highway Res. Board, 49th*, Highway Res. Board, Washington, D.C., 1969.

[4]   Brokke, G. E., and Mertz, W. L., Evaluating trip forecasting methods with an electronic computer. Highway Res. Bull. No. 203, pp. 52–75. Highway Res. Board, Washington, 1958.

[5]   Buchanan, C., ed., *Traffic in Towns*. HM Stationery Office, London, 1963.

[6]   Chicago Area Transportation Study, Final Rept., Vol. 2, Chicago, Illinois, 1960.

[7]   Dafermos, S. C., An extended traffic assignment model with applications to two-way traffic. *Transportation Science* **5**, 366–389 (1971); see also *Transportation Science* **6**, 73–87 (1972).

[8]   Ford, L. R., and Fulkerson, D. R., *Flows in Networks*. Princeton Univ. Press, Princeton, New Jersey, 1962.

[9]   Fratar, T. J., Forecasting distribution of interzonal vehicular trips by successive approximations. *Proceedings of Highway Research Board* **33**, 376–385 (1954).

[10]   Helly, W., Some techniques for the evaluation of ground service to air travellers. Rep. 63-5. Res. and Develop. Div., Port of New York Authority, New York, 1963.

[11]   *Highway Capacity Manual*. Special Rep. 87. Highway Res. Board, Washington, D.C., 1965.

[12]   Hillier, F. S., and Lieberman, G. J., *Introduction to Operations Research*, pp. 218–222. Holden-Day, San Francisco, California, 1968.

[13]   Hoel, P. G., *Introduction to Mathematical Statistics*. Wiley, New York, 1947.

[14]   Martin, B. V., *A Computer Program for Traffic Assignment Research*. Dept. of Civil Eng., MIT, Cambridge, Massachusetts, 1964.

[15]   Martin, B. V., *Minimum Path Algorithms for Transportation Planning*. Dept. of Civil Eng., MIT, Cambridge, Massachusetts, 1963.

[16]   *Pittsburgh Area Transportation Study*, Pittsburgh, Pennsylvania, 1961.

[17]   Potts, R. B., and Oliver, R. M., *Flows in Transportation Networks*. Academic Press, New York, 1972.

[18]   Pratt, R. H., A utilitarian theory of travel mode choice. *Annu. Meeting Highway Res. Board, 40th*, Highway Res. Board, Washington, D.C., 1970.

[19] *Queens-Long Island Traffic Demand Model.* Traffic Res. Corp., New York, 1968.

[20] Stopher, P. R., A probability model of travel mode choice for the journey to work. *Annu. Meeting Highway Res. Board, 48th,* Highway Res. Board, Washington, D.C., 1969.

[21] *Traffic Assignment Manual.* Bur. of Public Roads, Washington, D.C., 1964.

[22] Voorhees, A. M., A general theory of traffic movement. *Traffic Engineering, 1955,* **26,** pp. 46–56.

[23] Warner, S. L., *Stochastic Choice of Model in Urban Travel.* Northwestern Univ. Press, Evanston, Illinois, 1962.

[24] Whitaker, R. W., and Kent, K. E., The intervening opportunity model: A theoretical consideration. Highway Res. Board Record No. 250, pp. 1–8. Highway Res. Board, Washington, D.C., 1968.

[25] Wilson, A. G., A statistical theory of spatial distribution models. *Transportation Research* **1,** 253–269 (1967).

Chapter *6*

Congestion at Bottlenecks

6-1 Introduction

Congestion is perhaps the most prevalent and vexing problem of urban life. Some people view it as *the* urban disease. Patently, congestion is the result of excessive demand by customers for services by overtaxed facilities. Wherever there is congestion, some or all of the customers will be denied service or will queue up to wait until service is provided.

A few examples ought to be mentioned. People queue for services performed by other people at post offices, medical clinics, and civil or criminal courts. They queue for services performed by machines or by inanimate facilities, when they make phone calls, seek apartments, or compete for use of a limited number of public tennis courts. Seated in automobiles, they queue at toll plazas, intersections, parking areas, and rush hour "expressways." Fires queue to await fire fighters, and assaulted citizens queue for police aid. Ships queue at piers; airplanes "stack up" at airports; and checked baggage waits to be claimed.

In each of these cases, it is possible—in principle—to expand service capacity so as to exceed demand practically all of the time, thus virtually eliminating the expense and aggravation caused by congestion. However, the costs can be prohibitive. If so, the best that can be done is to organize, schedule, balance, or ration limited resources so as to cope with inevitable congestion in the most graceful and efficient way possible. To do so, it is useful to analyze the underlying queueing phenomena in sufficient depth to make possible quantitative comparisons of alternative operating strategies.

This chapter is rather more mathematical than the rest of the book. To ease matters, the methodology is explained at length, and some points are covered twice, first intuitively and then more rigorously.

6-2   Some Definitions and Observations

(a)   Definitions

Any queueing model is a composite description of three processes: customer arrivals, the queue behavior or "discipline," and the services provided to the customer. Here are some of the ways these processes can occur.

1. *Arrivals*   Customers arrive for service singly or in groups. The arrivals may be scheduled or they may occur at random, according to some probability distribution for the interarrival times. Arriving customers may join the queue system, or they may decide not to do so, presumably because they observe unacceptable congestion. Customers who choose not to join are said to "balk."

2. *Queue Discipline*   If arriving customers cannot be served immediately, they are said to be "blocked." In some systems, a blocked customer is thrown out or "cleared." For example, the service system consisting of one person, with one telephone, will clear newly arriving telephone calls (with "busy" signals) while any one telephone call is in progress. In some systems, there is limited waiting room for blocked customers, so that some of them may wait for service. However, when this limited waiting room is filled, newly blocked customers are cleared from the system. In still other systems, there is virtually unlimited waiting room. If a customer is allowed to wait, he perhaps may do so until he is served. Contrariwise, he may choose to quit the system, or "renege," at some time before receiving service. Waiting customers may be served in order of arrival, at random, or according to some priority scheme. They may even be served in inverse order of arrival.

3. *Service*   There may be one or more servers. Customers may enter service individually or in groups. For example, an elevator provides "bulk" service to groups of customers. The time taken by a server to handle a customer may be fixed, or it may be a random interval drawn from an appropriate probability distribution function.

Now consider a queue system with these more specific properties:

1.   Customers arrive for service at a mean rate of λ customers per unit

time. Then the mean time between arrivals is $1/\lambda$. For example, $\lambda = 10$ per hour implies a mean interarrival time interval of $1/\lambda = \frac{1}{10}$ hour.

2. All customers wait for service. They are served in order of arrival.

3. There are s servers. Each server handles one customer at a time. Let τ be the mean time required for one server to serve one customer. Let $\mu = 1/\tau$ be the mean rate at which one server can serve customers. Thus, if the mean service time is $\tau = \frac{1}{2}$ hour, one server can handle $\mu = 1/\tau = 2$ customers per hour. If there are $s = 6$ servers in the system, the system can handle $s\mu = s/\tau = 12$ customers per hour.

Let "1 Erlang" be that amount of customer traffic that keeps one server busy all the time. This traffic unit is named after A. K. Erlang, a notable pioneer in queueing theory. Let a be the number of Erlangs of traffic offered by the arriving customers. Thus, customers, arriving at a mean rate λ and each requiring a mean service time $\tau = 1/\mu$, offer the queue system a traffic volume of $a = \lambda\tau = \lambda/\mu$ Erlangs. For example, if $\lambda = 10$ per hour and $\tau = \frac{1}{2}$ hour, then $a = \lambda\tau = 5$ Erlangs. This offered traffic volume would keep five servers busy 100% of the time. If the system has s servers, it can handle a maximum of s Erlangs of traffic. Thus the fraction ρ, of system capacity actually used, is

$$\rho = a/s = \lambda\tau/s = \lambda/s\mu.$$

Alternatively, ρ may be viewed as the mean fraction of the time any one server is busy (provided all servers participate equally in the work). So, if $\lambda = 10$ per hour, $\tau = \frac{1}{2}$ hour, and $s = 8$, then $\rho = 0.625 =$ fraction of system capacity used $=$ mean fraction of time that any one server is busy.

Let $n(t)$ be the number of customers in the system at time t. Clearly, $n(t)$ must be an integer greater than or equal to zero. $n(t)$ includes both those customers who are waiting in the queue and those who are being served. Since both the interarrival times and the service times may be random variables, one usually cannot calculate $n(t)$ with certainty. One must be content with a probabilistic description of the system. To this end, let

$p_n(t) =$ probability that there are precisely n customers in the queue system at time t.

Since there is some number of customers, perhaps zero, in the system at any time, one must have

$$\sum_{n=0}^{\infty} P_n(t) = 1 \qquad (6\text{-}1)$$

for all moments in time.

The mean, or expected, number of customers in the system is defined as $E[n(t)]$, where

$$E[n(t)] = \sum_{n=0}^{\infty} n \cdot P_n(t). \tag{6-2}$$

This definition of the mean value is that generally used in probabilistic calculations. Thus, if at some time t, $P_0(t) = 0.2$, $P_1(t) = 0.4$, $P_2(t) = 0.2$, $P_3(t) = 0.2$, and $P_n(t) = 0$ for n bigger than 3, then

$$E[n(t)] = 0(0.2) + 1(0.4) + 2(0.2) + 3(0.2) = 1.4.$$

Let $q(n)$ be the number of customers waiting in the queue when there are n customers in the system. Note that, when there are less than s customers, all are being served by the s servers. However, when there are s or more customers, only s are being served, and the rest are in the queue. Thus, $q(n) = 0$ if $n < s$, and $q(n) = (n - s)$ if $n \geq s$. The expected number of customers in the queue is defined as $E[q(n)]$ where

$$E[q(n)] = \sum_{n=0}^{\infty} q(n)P_n = \sum_{n=s}^{\infty} (n - s)P_n, \tag{6-3}$$

and P_n is the probability that there are n customers in the system. So if as before $P_0 = 0.2$, $P_1 = 0.4$, $P_2 = 0.2$, $P_3 = 0.2$, and $P_n = 0$ for all other n, and if now we set $s = 1$ server, then

$$E[q(n)] = \sum_{n=1}^{\infty} (n - 1)P_n = 0(0.4) + 1(0.2) + 2(0.2) = 0.6.$$

(b) Oversaturated Systems

If the traffic offered to the system, $a = \lambda_T$ Erlangs, is greater than the maximum traffic the system can handle, s Erlangs, then the system is oversaturated and cannot keep up with the demand for service. Note that this condition, $a > s$, is equivalent to

$$a/s = \lambda_T/s = \rho > 1;$$

so the average occupancy demanded of a server is greater than 1. This is impossible; so the queue of waiting customers will grow and grow as time progresses.

Under these circumstances, it is a reasonable approximation to assume that all s servers will be busy all the time. While this may not be true for occasional moments when the service is faster than average, the excess of customer demand over service capability will ensure it practically all the time. On the basis of this assumption, one can immediately write down an equation for the expected rate of growth in the number of customers. Since $n(t)$ is the number in the system, $dn(t)/dt$ is the rate of growth of this number, and $E[dn(t)/dt]$ is the expected ($=$ mean) rate of growth. Clearly,

$$E\left[\frac{dn(t)}{dt}\right] = E[\text{arrival rate of customers into the system}]$$

$$-E\left[\begin{array}{l}\text{departure rate of customers, approximated} \\ \text{by the service rate when all servers are busy}\end{array}\right].$$

Since the mean arrival rate is λ and the mean service rate, when all servers are busy, is $s\mu$, one obtains

$$E\left[\frac{dn(t)}{dt}\right] = \lambda - s\mu, \tag{6-4}$$

where μ is the service rate for a busy server, $\mu = 1/\tau$. If both λ and μ are constants, then $E[dn(t)/dt]$ is a positive constant for our oversaturated system; so the expected number in the system increases linearly with time:

$$E[n(t)] = n(t = 0) + (\lambda - s\mu)t. \tag{6-5}$$

Equation (6-4) offers a reasonable approximation for the time-dependent behavior of a grossly oversaturated system. For an application, see Problem 2 in the Problems section.

(c)   Statistical Equilibrium

If the offered traffic, $a = \lambda\tau$ Erlangs, is less than the s Erlangs that the system can handle, then $(\lambda\tau/s) < 1$, and the system is said to be unsaturated. There still can be waiting customers, perhaps even most of the time, because of flurries of irregular arrivals or above-average service times. However, now, because the service capacity exceeds demand, the expected queue size will not grow without limit. In this situation, there is a possibility that the probabilities $P_n(t)$, for n customers in the system, may not depend on time. If $P_n(t)$ does not vary with time, then $dP_n(t)/dt = 0$; so one can write $P_n(t) = P_n$. Furthermore, Eqs. (6-2) and (6-3) simplify to

$$E(n) = \sum_{n=0}^{\infty} nP_n \quad \text{and} \quad E[q(n)] = \sum_{n=s}^{\infty} (n - s)P_n. \tag{6-6}$$

If a system evolves indefinitely in time with $dP_n(t)/dt = 0$, it is said to be in *statistical equilibrium*.

If a system is unsaturated and if both arrival and service rates do not vary with time, then the system will evolve toward statistical equilibrium as time progresses. This is a most important property of queue systems, which the reader will have to accept without proof because a general demonstration is a rather subtle and difficult project.

Mathematical analysis is much easier for statistical equilibrium than it is for time-dependent behavior. Hence it is usual to make detailed studies of queues in statistical equilibrium, a feasible situation whenever $\rho = (\lambda \tau / s) < 1$, even if the real systems being modeled are not quite in statistical equilibrium. Fortunately, many real systems are in approximate equilibrium for usefully long periods of time.

(d)   The Expected Waiting Time

Consider a queue system in statistical equilibrium. Let $E(w_q)$ be the mean, or expected, waiting time spent by customers in the queue. It will now be shown that

$$E(w_q) = E(q)/\lambda, \tag{6-7}$$

where $E(q) = E[q(n)] =$ the expected number of customers in the queue, as given by Eqs. (6-6).

The following argument supporting Eq. (6-7) is due to Burke [5]. Consider a long time interval, of length T, during which statistical equilibrium prevails:

(i)   During the interval T, customers arrive at a mean rate λ; so the expected number of arrivals is λT. The expected waiting time of an arrival is $E(w_q)$; so the expected sum of waiting times for all arrivals is $\lambda T E(w_q)$.

(ii)   During the time interval T, the mean number of customers in the queue is $E(q)$. Therefore, the expected total time, spent by all customers waiting in the queue, is $E(q)T$.

(iii)   As $T \rightarrow \infty$, the expected sum of the waiting times, suffered by arriving customers, must equal the expected sum of the times spent waiting in the queue. Hence

$$\lim_{T \to \infty} \lambda T E(w_q) = \lim_{T \to \infty} E(q) T.$$

Equation (6-7) follows directly from this.

A completely parallel argument can be used to show that

$$E(w) = E(n)/\lambda, \tag{6-8}$$

where $E(w)$ is the mean total time spent in the system by customers, and $E(n)$ is the mean number of customers as exhibited in Eqs. (6-6).

6-3   A Single-Server Queue

This section offers a somewhat intuitive analysis of a single-server queue in statistical equilibrium. It is intended to serve as a curtain raiser to the more thorough and general presentation which follows it. Suppose that customers arrive singly at a mean rate of λ customers per unit time. If a customer arrives when the queue system is empty, he immediately enters service. If there are one or more customers already there, the new customer joins the queue, waits until he is first, and then is served. After he is served, the customer leaves the system.

Let τ be the mean time taken by the server to serve one customer. Then $\mu = 1/\tau$ is the mean rate at which customers are served while the server is busy. For statistical equilibrium to exist, we require that $a = (\lambda/\mu) < 1$, where a is the traffic offered to the system. Note that, since the number of servers $s = 1$, the mean server occupancy $\rho = (a/s) = a$.

The queue system is characterized by its state n, where n is the number of customers it contains. This number will increase by one whenever a customer arrives, and it will decrease by one whenever a customer departs. Figure 6-1 shows the possible states of the system and the transitions between states that may occur. Arrows pointing to the right, e.g., from n to $(n + 1)$, show possible arrival transitions. Arrows pointing to the left show possible departure transitions.

Because the queue system is assumed to be in statistical equilibrium, the probabilities P_n of the system having n customers in it are independent of time.

We now find the expected number of transitions into state n during a long time interval of length T:

(a)   A transition into state n occurs when the system is in state $(n - 1)$ and a customer arrives. P_{n-1} is the probability of state $(n - 1)$ and there-

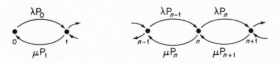

FIG. 6-1   A Single-Server Queue System in Equilibrium

fore is the expected fraction of the total time that the system is in state $(n - 1)$. Therefore, during T, the expected time in state $(n - 1)$ is $P_{n-1}T$. The mean arrival rate is λ, and so the expected number of arrivals during T, while the system is in state $(n - 1)$, is $\lambda P_{n-1}T$.

(b)   A transition into state n occurs when the system is in state $(n + 1)$ and a customer finishes service and leaves. During T, the expected time in state $(n + 1)$ is $P_{n+1}T$. The mean service completion rate is μ, and so the expected number of departures during T, while the system is in state $(n + 1)$, is $\mu P_{n+1}T$.

Hence the expected number of transitions, into state n during T, is $(\lambda P_{n-1} + \mu P_{n+1})T$.

The expected number of transitions, out of state n during T, can be found in the same way. During T, the expected time in state n is P_nT. The mean arrival rate is λ, and the mean service rate is μ; so the expected number of transitions, out of state n during T, is $(\lambda + \mu)P_nT$.

Consider the system as $T \to \infty$. Because P_n is independent of time, the expected number of transitions into state n must equal the expected number of transitions out of state n. If this were not so, the probability that the system is in state n would increase or decrease as time progresses. Hence

$$\lim_{T \to \infty} \left[(\lambda P_{n-1} + \mu P_{n+1})T \right] = \lim_{T \to \infty} \left[(\lambda + \mu)P_nT) \right];$$

so

$$\lambda P_{n-1} + \mu P_{n+1} = (\lambda + \mu)P_n, \quad \text{for} \quad n = 1, 2, 3, \ldots. \quad (6\text{-}9)$$

Consider now the somewhat special case of $n = 0$. Because there can be no departures from an empty system and because the state $n = -1$ does not exist, two of the terms in Eq. (6-9) do not occur, and the equilibrium equation becomes

$$\mu P_1 = \lambda P_0. \quad (6\text{-}10)$$

From Eq. (6-10),

$$P_1 = (\lambda/\mu)P_0 = \rho P_0,$$

where $\rho = (\lambda/\mu)$. From Eq. (6-9):

$$P_2 = (1/\mu)[(\lambda + \mu)P_1 - \lambda P_0] = (\lambda/\mu)^2 P_0 = \rho^2 P_0$$

$$P_3 = (1/\mu)[(\lambda + \mu)P_2 - \lambda P_1] = (\lambda/\mu)^2 P_1 = \rho^3 P_0$$

$$\vdots$$

$$P_n = (\lambda/\mu)^n P_0 = \rho^n P_0. \quad (6\text{-}11)$$

P_0 can be found by using Eq. (6-1), which expresses the fact that the system always is in some state:

$$\sum_{n=0}^{\infty} P_n = 1.$$

Thus

$$P_0 + \sum_{n=1}^{\infty} \rho^n P_0 = P_0 \left(1 + \sum_{n=1}^{\infty} \rho^n\right) = P_0 \sum_{n=0}^{\infty} \rho^n = 1,$$

and

$$P_0 = \left[\sum_{n=0}^{\infty} \rho^n\right]^{-1} = (1 - \rho);$$

so

$$P_n = (1 - \rho)\rho^n, \quad \text{for} \quad n = 0, 1, 2, \ldots. \tag{6-12}$$

The mean number of customers in the system, $E(n)$, and the mean number of customers in the queue, $E(q)$, were defined by Eq. (6-6) as

$$E(n) = \sum_{n=0}^{\infty} n P_n \quad \text{and} \quad E(q) = \sum_{n=1}^{\infty} (n - 1) P_n.$$

Substituting from Eq. (6-12) and simplifying, one finds

$$E(n) = \rho/(1 - \rho) \tag{6-13}$$

and

$$E(q) = \rho^2/(1 - \rho). \tag{6-14}$$

The mean time in the system, $E(w)$, and the mean time in the queue, $E(w_q)$, were shown in Eqs. (6-7) and (6-8) to be

$$E(w) = E(n)/\lambda = \rho/\lambda(1 - \rho) = 1/(\mu - \lambda) \tag{6-15}$$

and

$$E(w_q) = E(q)/\lambda = \rho^2/\lambda(1 - \rho) = \lambda/u(\mu - \lambda). \tag{6-16}$$

These results are illustrated in Table 6-1, wherein the mean service time is taken to be $\tau = 1/u = 1$ minute. Various arrival rates are compared, and it should be noted how delays increase enormously as saturation is approached.

It will be shown in the next section that the queue system model shown here implies that the time intervals between arrivals are drawn from an

TABLE 6-1
Numerical Illustrations for a Single-Server Queue[a]

	λ = mean arrival rate in customers per minute = ρ = mean server occupancy				
	0.01	0.1	0.0	0.9	0.99
P_0 = probability that system is empty, from Eq. (6-12)	0.99	0.9	0.5	0.1	0.01
$E(n)$ = mean number in the system, from Eq. (6-13)	0.0101	0.1111	1.0	9.0	99.0
$E[q(n)]$ = mean number in the queue, from Eq. (6-14)	0.0001	0.0111	0.5	8.1	98.01
$E(w)$ = mean time in system, in minutes, from Eq. (6-15)	1.0101	1.1111	2.0	10.0	100.0
$E(w_q)$ = mean time in queue, in minutes, from Eq. (6-16)	0.0101	0.1111	1.0	9.0	99.0

[a] The queue system described is characterized by exponentially distributed interarrival times, exponentially distributed service times, and a mean service time $\tau = 1$ minute.

exponential distribution, with parameter λ, for which

$$\Pr(T_a > t) = \text{probability that the interarrival time } T_a \text{ is greater than a specified time } t$$

$$= e^{-\lambda t}.$$

The service times also are distributed exponentially, but with parameter μ; so

$$\Pr(T_s > t) = \text{probability that the service time } T_s \text{ is greater than a specified time } t$$

$$= e^{-\mu t}.$$

6-4 The Birth and Death Equation Applied to Queue Systems

In Chapter 2, a birth and death equation was developed for describing the size of a population as a function of time. This equation will be presented again here, now with the viewpoint that births represent arrivals, deaths represent departures, and the population size represents the number of customers in the queue system. In the queueing context, the birth and death equation is the direct consequence of assuming a Poisson probability distribution to describe customer arrivals and an exponential probability distribution to describe the service times.

Because some readers may not be fully prepared for the mathematics of this section, we first summarize the results of the derivations that follow. This summary may well suffice as a basis for the subsequent material. However, it would be most desirable for the reader to study the entire section.

Section (a) below shows that, if customers arrive at a queue system independently in such a way that the probability of an arrival at any moment is independent of any prior or subsequent arrivals, then the probability $P_n(t)$ of n arrivals during a time interval t is given by the Poisson distribution,

$$P_n(t) = (\lambda t)^n e^{-\lambda t}/n!,$$

where λ is the mean number of arrivals per unit time. It is shown also that the time intervals between such arrivals are distributed exponentially; so the probability is $e^{-\lambda t}$ that the interval is greater than t.

Section (b) proposes the use of an exponential distribution for the length of time one server requires to serve one customer. The distribution is given by $\Pr(\text{service time} > t) = e^{-\mu t}$, where $(1/\mu)$ is the mean service time. μ is the mean rate at which one server can serve customers.

Section (c) develops birth and death equation (6-23) for the probabilities $P_n(t)$ of there being n customers in the system at time t. The equations are based on λ_n being defined as the mean arrival rate and μ_n being defined as the mean service rate, when there are n customers in the system. The arguments used in obtaining these equations are appropriate for Poisson arrivals and exponentially distributed service times, provided λ_n and μ_n are properly defined and interpreted, as will be done in the following sections.

Section (d) derives the solution to the birth and death equation in the case of statistical equilibrium, where $dP_n(t)/dt = 0$ for all n. The solution is shown, in Eq. (6-26), to be

$$P_n = \left[\frac{\lambda_{n-1}\lambda_{n-2}\lambda_{n-3}\cdots\lambda_0}{\mu_n\mu_{n-1}\mu_{n-2}\cdots\mu_1}\right] P_0,$$

where P_0 can be found from

$$\sum_{n=0}^{\infty} P_n = 1.$$

(a) Poisson Arrivals

Assume that the probability $P_n(t)$ of n customer arrivals in a time t is given by

$$P_n(t) = (\lambda t)^n e^{-\lambda t}/n!. \tag{6-17}$$

Equation (6-17) is known as the Poisson distribution. The expected number of arrivals during the time t is

$$E(n) = \sum_{n=0}^{\infty} nP_n(t) = \lambda t,$$

so that λ is the mean arrival rate in customers per unit time. It follows that $(1/\lambda) = \tau$ is the mean time between arrivals.

Let T be the time interval between two arrivals. The probability that T is greater than any specified time t is given by $P_0(t)$ = the probability that no one arrives during t:

$$\Pr(T > t) = P_0(t) = e^{-\lambda t}. \tag{6-18}$$

Equation (6-18) describes an exponential probability distribution and shows that this exponential distribution applies to the time intervals between arrivals with a Poisson distribution.

A remarkable property of the exponential distribution is its "lack of memory." To show this, let $\Pr(T > t + h \mid T > t)$ be the probability that the exponentially distributed time interval T is greater than $t + h$, given that it is greater than t. It is axiomatic in probability theory that

$$\Pr(T > t + h \mid T > t) \cdot \Pr(T > t) = \Pr(T > t + h).$$

Using Eq. (6-18), one obtains

$$\Pr(T > t + h \mid T > t) = \frac{\Pr(T > t + h)}{\Pr(T > t)} = \frac{e^{-\lambda(t+h)}}{e^{-\lambda t}} = e^{-\lambda h}. \tag{6-19}$$

Equation (6-19) shows that $\Pr(T > t + h \mid T > t)$ is independent of t. Thus, no matter how long a time t an exponentially distributed interval has been in progress, the remaining time for that interval is a random number drawn from the original distribution. Only the exponential distribution has this lack of memory of the time when an interval started.

Since the Poisson arrival process has exponentially distributed interarrival times, any time t during the arrival process is a time set during an exponential interarrival interval. Because of the lack of memory property, the interval, from that arbitrary time t until the next arrival, is distributed exponentially. Hence the probability of no arrival during an infinitesimal

dt is $e^{-\lambda\,dt}$, regardless of when the interval dt starts. So

$$\Pr(\text{no arrival in } dt) = \Pr(T > dt) = e^{-\lambda\,dt}.$$

The exponential can be expanded in a power series:

$$\Pr(\text{no arrival in } dt) = e^{-\lambda\,dt} = 1 - \lambda\,dt + \frac{(\lambda\,dt)^2}{2!} - \frac{(\lambda\,dt)^3}{3!} + \cdots.$$

In the limit as dt approaches zero,

$$\lim_{dt\to 0}\Pr(\text{no arrival in } dt) = 1 - \lambda\,dt + o(dt^2). \tag{6-20a}$$

Here $o(dt^2)$ is a symbol for any function that approaches zero at least as fast as dt^2 when dt approaches zero. The probability that the next arrival occurs during dt is

$$\Pr(\text{arrival in } dt) = 1 - \Pr(\text{no arrival in } dt);$$

so

$$\lim_{dt\to 0}\Pr(\text{arrival in } dt) = \lambda\,dt + o(dt^2). \tag{6-20b}$$

Finally, it is reasonable to claim, and it can be proved, that

$$\lim_{dt\to 0}\Pr(\text{two or more arrivals in } dt) = o(dt^2). \tag{6-20c}$$

The main thing that has been shown here about Poisson arrivals is in Eq. (6-20b), which says that the probability of an arrival in any short dt is proportional to the size of dt and does not depend at all on when earlier arrivals occurred. It is for this reason that Poisson arrivals are sometimes called "pure random" arrivals. The distribution is most important and useful because many real congestion situations are characterized by arrival processes that are at least approximately Poisson.

(b) Exponentially Distributed Service Times

The probability $P(T_s > t)$ that the service time T_s exceeds a given specific time t is assumed to be exponential with parameter μ; so $P(T_s > t) = e^{-\mu t}$. The mean service time for this distribution is $\tau = 1/\mu$; so μ may be viewed as the mean rate of service by a busy server.†

---

† The density function of the exponential distribution is $f(t) = \mu e^{-\mu t}$; so the expected value τ of the time is $\int_0^\infty t f(t)\,dt = 1/\mu$.

The same argument, used for exponentially distributed arrival times, can be used to show that, if a customer is being served at the beginning of an infinitesimal dt,

$$\lim_{dt \to 0} \mathrm{Pr}(\text{service does not end in } dt) = 1 - \mu\, dt + o(dt^2)$$

$$\lim_{dt \to 0} \mathrm{Pr}(\text{service ends in } dt) = \mu\, dt + o(dt^2)$$

$$\lim_{dt \to 0} \mathrm{Pr}\binom{\text{two or more customers}}{\text{complete service in } dt} = o(dt^2). \tag{6-21}$$

Now suppose that j servers are busy, each independently serving one customer. Suppose each of the service times is drawn from the same exponential distribution with parameter μ. Because the servers are independent of one another,

$$\mathrm{Pr}\binom{\text{none of the } j \text{ servers}}{\text{completes service in } dt} = \left[\mathrm{Pr}\begin{pmatrix}\text{any one of the } j\\ \text{servers does not}\\ \text{end service in } dt\end{pmatrix} \right]^{j}.$$

It follows that

$$\lim_{dt \to 0} \mathrm{Pr}\binom{\text{none of the } j \text{ servers}}{\text{completes service in } dt} = \begin{array}{l}[1 - \mu\, dt + o(dt^2)]^j\\ = 1 - j\mu\, dt + o(dt^2),\end{array} \tag{6-22a}$$

from which it follows that

$$\lim_{dt \to 0} \mathrm{Pr}\binom{\text{one of the } j \text{ servers}}{\text{completes service in } dt} = j\mu\, dt + o(dt^2), \tag{6-22b}$$

and

$$\lim_{dt \to 0} \mathrm{Pr}\binom{\text{two or more of } j \text{ servers}}{\text{complete service in } dt} = o(dt^2). \tag{6-22c}$$

These probabilities, Eqs. (6-22), have the same form as for a single server; only now the probability of a service completion in dt is j times as big as for one server.

An interesting observed fact is that ordinary personal telephone calls have approximately exponentially distributed durations. Unfortunately, most other services do not adhere to this distribution. Nevertheless, it is used for much queue system analysis because

(a)   the mathematics turns out to be fairly easy, and

(b)   the real service time distribution often is not sufficiently different to yield very different results.

(c)   The State Equations

Let

n = the number of customers in the system. Usually, n is called the "state" of the system,

$P_n(t)$ = the probability that there are n customers in the system at time t,

λ_n = the mean rate of customer arrivals when the system contains n customers,

μ_n = the mean rate at which the customers are served when the system contains n customers.

Assume that the distributions of interarrival times and of service times are exponential. Then the probabilities of arrivals or departures, during a small dt, are given by Eqs. (6-20) and (6-21), now modified with the subscript n to provide for possibly different rates in different system states. These probabilities are exactly the same as those postulated for births and deaths in a population, as shown in Chapter 2, Eqs. (2-2). It is demonstrated there that the consequent "birth and death" equations, for the state probabilities $P_n(t)$, are

$$\frac{dP_n(t)}{dt} = \lambda_{n-1}P_{n-1}(t) + \mu_{n+1}P_{n+1}(t) - (\lambda_n + \mu_n)P_n(t). \quad (6\text{-}23)$$

Equation (6-23) is the same as Eq. (2-3), except that now λ_n and μ_n are constants independent of time.

(d)   Statistical Equilibrium

If the state probabilities are independent of time, then $dP_n(t)/dt = 0$ and Eq. (6-23) reduces to

$$0 = \lambda_{n-1}P_{n-1} + \lambda_{n+1}P_{n+1} - (\lambda_n + \mu_n)P_n. \quad (6\text{-}24)$$

Since no departure is possible from an empty system, $\mu_0 = 0$. Also, there cannot be a negative number of customers; so $P_{-1} = 0$. Therefore, the following special equation holds for $n = 0$:

$$0 = \mu_1 P_1 - \lambda_0 P_0. \quad (6\text{-}25)$$

Equations (6-24) and (6-25) can be solved recursively to yield

$$P_n = \left(\frac{\lambda_{n-1}\lambda_{n-2}\lambda_{n-3}\cdots\lambda_0}{\mu_n\mu_{n-1}\mu_{n-2}\cdots\mu_1} \right) P_0. \quad (6\text{-}26)$$

Once all the P_n's are known in terms of P_0, P_0 can be found from

$$\sum_{n=0}^{\infty} P_n = 1.$$

6-5   The S-Server Queue System

This section derives results and exhibits examples for a system in equilibrium with Poisson arrivals, a single queue, and exponentially distributed service times provided by S servers.

(a)   Theory

If a queue system is served by more than one server, there are two main ways to organize the queue discipline:

1.   Each server has his own queue, and customers do not switch from one queue to another. This is equivalent to several single-server queues, each of which can be analyzed by the model of Section 6.3. The approach has the disadvantage that a server may be idle, while one or more customers are in line for other servers.

2.   A single queue is served by all the servers in the system. This is more efficient and is the approach taken by most multiserver systems. For example, if one supermarket checkout counter becomes idle, customers will switch to it from queues at other counters. Thus, while first-come first-served discipline will not be maintained at the market, the queue system still maintains the overall advantage of a single queue served by the several servers.

It is quite easy to apply the birth and death formalism to a system that consists of one queue served by S servers. Assume that the mean customer arrival rate λ is independent of the number of customers already in the system. Assume further that all customers remain for service. Then

$$\lambda_n = \text{mean arrival rate, given } n \text{ customers in system,}$$

$$= \lambda, \quad \text{for all} \quad n \geq 0.$$

If the mean time taken by one server to serve one customer is $1/\mu$, then the mean rate of serving customers is μ for one busy server, 2μ for two busy servers, and so on up to $S\mu$ for S busy servers. Thus, if the number of customers is less than, or equal to, the number of servers, all customers will be in service; so

μ_n = mean service rate, given n customers in system,

$= n\mu,$ for $0 \leq n \leq S.$

When there are S or more customers in the system, S customers will be in service, and the rest will be waiting in the queue; so

$$\mu_n = S\mu, \quad \text{for} \quad n \geq S.$$

If these values of λ_n and μ_n are substituted into the statistical equilibrium solution (6-26) for the birth and death equation, one obtains

P_n = probability that there are n customers in the system

$= (1/n!) (\lambda/\mu)^n P_0$ for $0 \leq n \leq S$

$= (1/S! S^{n-S}) (\lambda/\mu)^n P_0$ for $n \geq S.$ (6-27a)

Now P_0 can be found by substituting Eqs. (6-27a) into $\sum_{n=0}^{\infty} P_n = 1$. After some simplification, one obtains

$$P_0 = \left[\sum_{n=0}^{S-1} \frac{1}{n!} \left(\frac{\lambda}{\mu} \right)^n + \frac{1}{S!} \left(\frac{\lambda}{\mu} \right)^S \left(\frac{S\mu}{S\mu - \lambda} \right) \right]^{-1}. \quad (6\text{-}27\text{b})$$

It was shown, Eq. (6-6), that the mean number of customers waiting in the queue is

$$E(q) = \sum_{n=S}^{\infty} (n - S) P_n.$$

Substitution of Eq. (6-27a) into this expression yields

$$E(q) = \frac{\rho (\lambda/\mu)^S P_0}{S! (1 - \rho)^2}, \quad (6\text{-}28)$$

where $\rho = (\lambda/S\mu)$ is the traffic volume per server in Erlangs. The mean waiting time is given by Eq. (6-7):

$$E(w_q) = E(q)/\lambda. \quad (6\text{-}29)$$

The mean time $E(w)$, spent by a customer in the system, is the mean waiting time plus the mean service time $(1/\mu)$; so

$$E(w) = E(w_q) + 1/\mu = E(q)/\lambda + 1/\mu. \quad (6\text{-}30)$$

(b)   Example 1: Outpatient Clinics

Middletown proposes to set up either one or two clinics to provide community health care for its poorer citizens. The budget is sufficient for two doctors; so if one clinic is set up, the clinic will have two servers. If two clinics are set up, each clinic will have one server. It is anticipated that service for most minor complaints will be on a walk-in (no appointments) basis and that the average time required of a doctor to serve one patient will be $\frac{1}{4}$ hour. Thus, the mean service rate, for one occupied doctor, is expected to be $\mu = 4$ per hour. The overall patient arrival rate λ_t is expected to be the same for either the one-clinic or the two-clinic setup.

The problem is to decide between the one-clinic and the two-clinic setups on the basis of which one yields smaller patient delays. It will be assumed that patients arrive in a Poisson process and that service times are distributed exponentially.

(1) *Simpleminded Analysis*   If there are to be two clinics, each one will consist of a single-server system, $S = 1$. In this case, Eqs. (6-27b) and (6-29) reduce to

$$P_0 = 1 - \rho, \qquad E(w_q) = \rho^2/\lambda(1 - \rho) = \rho/\mu(1 - \rho),$$

where $\rho = (\lambda/\mu)$. These relationships were derived previously in Section 6.3. Since each of the single-server systems will handle half the total traffic λ_t, $\lambda = \lambda_t/2$; so $\rho = (\lambda/\mu) = (\lambda_t/2\mu)$.

If there is to be one clinic, it will operate as a two-server system, $S = 2$. Then Eqs. (6-27b) and (6-29) reduce to

$$P_0 = (1 - \rho)/(1 + \rho), \qquad E(w_q) = \rho^2/[\mu(1 - \rho)(1 + \rho)]$$

where $\rho = (\lambda/S\mu) = (\lambda/2\mu)$. Because now the one system handles the total traffic λ_t, $\rho = (\lambda_t/2\mu)$. Note that ρ, being the mean server occupancy, is the same for both the two-clinic and the one-clinic setups. There can be equilibrium only if the mean server occupancy ρ is less than 1. Thus, for the given service rate $\mu = 4$ per server per hour, λ_t must be less than 8 per hour.

Figure 6-2 shows the mean waiting times $E(w_q)$, for both alternatives, plotted as functions of the overall customer arrival rate λ_t. It is seen that the single two-doctor clinic offers smaller mean delays for all equilibrium values of λ_t.

(2) *A More Sophisticated Analysis*   Patients must travel to a clinic before joining the queue system. If there are two clinics, suitably located, the mean travel time would be shorter than with one clinic. So it may well be that, if one compares the alternatives on the basis of combined travel and waiting times, the two-clinic setup may turn out to have a smaller

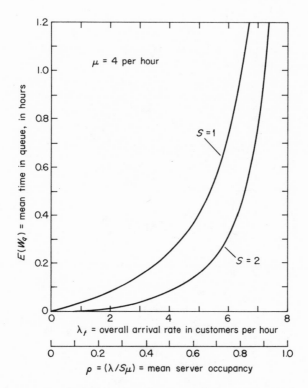

FIG. 6-2   Comparison of Mean Waiting Times: Single Server versus Two Servers with
Same Mean Server Occupancy

mean overall delay for service. To illustrate, suppose that the mean patient travel time is 0.5 hour, if there is only one clinic, and 0.3 hour if there are two clinics. Figure 6-3 shows the mean total (travel plus waiting) times for the two setups, given this assumption. It is seen that now the two-clinic setup is better for light traffic, $\lambda_t < 4.4$ customers per hour. The one-clinic setup remains better for $\lambda_t > 4.4$ customers per hour.

(c)   Example 2: Business District Street Parking

Consider the case of a downtown commercial area, typified by New York City's garment district. Such an area is host to a steady stream of commercial vehicles, which must appear and must be parked in order that loading and other requisite business activities be conducted. Such vehicles cannot be satisfied by remote parking facilities; hence they seek space

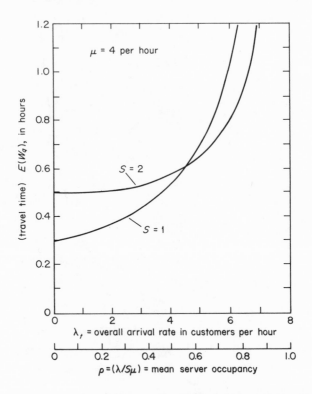

FIG. 6-3 Comparison of Mean Travel plus Waiting Times: Single Server versus
Two Servers (see text)

immediately in front of or adjoining their destinations. If the area predates
the modern truck era, most vehicles must use the streets for parking. Under
these conditions, the neighborhood searched by a single vehicle is quite
small, with curbside parking space for only a few vehicles. Call such a
neighborhood a "demand area."

Assume that vehicles, demanding parking space within one demand area,
arrive at random, with mean number λ arriving per unit time and exponential interarrival times. Assume further that they park a mean time $(1/\mu)$,
with exponentially distributed parking times. Let S be the number of
parking spaces in the demand area. A new customer (vehicle) will be
served at once if one of the S servers is idle (vacant). If not, the new customer joins the queue by cruising around the block or by double parking.
While thus in the queue, the new customer uses more street space than he
would while in service. Let R be the ratio of space required by a moving
(or double-parked) vehicle to the space required by a parked vehicle.

If the unit of area is taken to be the space required by one parked vehicle, the area required for the S-server parking spaces is S, and the area required by a queue of q waiting customers is Rq. The mean, or expected, ground area required by the system is

$$G = S + RE(q),$$

where $E(q)$ is the mean number of vehicles in the queue. $E(q)$ can be found from Eq. (6-28) since the system is a single queue with S servers. Note that in Eq. (6-28) the total traffic volume is $(\lambda/\mu) = a$, and the mean server occupancy is $\rho = (a/S)$.

For any given traffic volume a, the total required ground space G will vary with the number S of parking spaces provided. If S is less than a, there cannot be equilibrium, and the queue will grow indefinitely. If S is only slightly larger than a, the queue will use excessive space (and money for drivers). At the other extreme, if S is very large, the servers will waste space. On very crowded business district streets, one seeks to minimize the total space needed, and so the problem is to find the value of S that minimizes ground space G.

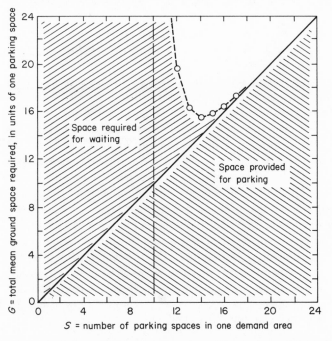

FIG. 6-4   Total Space Required as Function of Space Devoted to Parking

To illustrate, let

$a = 10$ Erlangs = traffic volume in one demand area,
$R = 3$ = ratio of space required by a vehicle in the queue to space required by a vehicle in service.

To find the optimum S, the required mean space G was calculated for $S = 10, 11, 12, \ldots$. The results are shown in Fig. 6-4. To understand the figure, consider the case of $S = 12$. From Eq. (6-28), for $a = 12\rho = 10$ Erlangs and $S = 12$, one obtains $E(q) = 2.5$. Hence $G = S + RE(q) = 12 + 3(2.5) = 19.5$, in units of one parking space area. In the figure, it is made clear that 12 units are needed for the servers and 7.5 units are needed for the queue.

The optimum number of parking spaces is seen to be 14. If the streets seem crowded when 14 spaces are provided per demand area, the classic reaction would be to reduce the number of parking spaces, thus liberating street space for an increased maximum apparent traffic volume. However, as can be seen from the figure, such a reduction of parking space would, of itself, generate additional, nonproductive traffic and would actually decrease the effective maximum traffic volume because there would be a smaller net residue of street space for through traffic.

(d) Example 3: Self-Service at the County Jail

The Metropole County Jail has a policy of accepting all persons arrested in Metropole, even if the jail is overcrowded. New customers are arrested, individually at random moments in time, in a Poisson process at a mean rate of $\lambda = 6$ customers per day. The time that an arrested person spends being served by the jail is drawn from an exponential distribution with a mean time $(1/\mu) = 4$ days. It is desired to make the capacity of the jail big enough so that the probability of overcrowding is less than 5% at any time. What should be the capacity of the jail?

The solution to this problem can be found by a simple extension of the S-server queueing model. Since the jail is prepared to accept all customers, without anyone ever waiting in a queue, it acts as though each customer serves himself, thus ensuring that there never is a shortage of servers.

Another way to view this service process is to postulate an infinite number of servers; so another idle server is always at hand to take on a new customer, no matter how many customers already are in jail. If thus $S = \infty$, Eqs. (6-27a) and (6-27b) reduce to

$$P_n = (1/n!)\,(\lambda/\mu)^n P_0$$

and

$$P_0 = \left[\sum_{n=0}^{\infty} (1/n!)(\lambda/\mu)^n\right]^{-1} = e^{-(\lambda/\mu)}.$$

Thus the probability that there are n customers in the jail is

$$P_n = (1/n!)(\lambda/\mu)^n e^{-(\lambda/\mu)}. \tag{6-31}$$

This is a Poisson distribution with mean value $E(n) = (\lambda/\mu)$.

The particular problem at hand has $\lambda = 6$ per day and $(1/\mu) = 4$ days; so $(\lambda/\mu) = 24 =$ mean number of customers in the jail. We seek the minimum jail capacity n_c with the property that the probability of more prisoners than n_c is less than 0.05. In mathematical terms, we seek the smallest n_c that satisfies

$$0.05 \geq \sum_{n=n_c}^{\infty} P_n = \sum_{n=n_c}^{\infty} (24)^n e^{-24}/n!.$$

Any table of the cumulative Poisson distribution will show that $n_c = 33$. Possibly the best table is to be found in Reference [4].

6-6   Limited Waiting Room

This section derives results and exhibits examples for a system in equilibrium with Poisson arrivals, a single queue with limited waiting room, and exponentially distributed service times provided by S servers. When the limited waiting room is fully occupied, newly arriving customers are not allowed to join and wait for service. Instead, they are "cleared" from the system and leave at once. It should be noted that, when there is limited waiting room, the queue cannot grow in size beyond the available maximum. Hence equilibrium is possible even when the arrival rate exceeds the maximum service rate.

(a)   Theory

The S-server queue methodology is modified only slightly if the queue system has limited waiting room. Suppose that the maximum number of customers, both waiting and being served, is N. Then, as in Section 6-5, $\lambda_n = \lambda =$ mean arrival rate with n customers in the system, as long as $n < N$. However, when $n = N$, $\lambda_n = \lambda_N = 0$, and newly arriving customers are not accepted. They are said to be "cleared" from the system. There is no modification to the service rates described in Section 6-5. So Eq. (6-27a) is modified only by $P_n = 0$ for $n > N$:

$$P_n = \text{probability that there are } n \text{ customers in the system}$$

$$= (1/n!)(\lambda/\mu)^n P_0 \qquad \text{for} \quad 0 \leqq n \leqq S$$

$$= (1/S!S^{n-S})(\lambda/\mu)^n P_0 \qquad \text{for} \quad S \leqq n \leqq N$$

$$= 0 \qquad \text{for} \quad n > N. \qquad (6\text{-}32a)$$

Since the maximum number of customers in the system is N, P_0 can be found from

$$\sum_{n=0}^{N} P_n = 1. \qquad (6\text{-}32b)$$

Now there is no efficient way to exhibit P_0 for all cases, as was done in Section 6.5 where $N = \infty$ led to Eq. (6-27b).

(b) *Example 1: Emergency Phone Service*

Middletown's police department has a phone-answering service for police and ambulance emergencies. Only $S = 1$ dispatcher is available to serve incoming phone calls. This dispatcher is to be equipped with a switchboard providing N incoming telephone lines. If a call arrives while the dispatcher is talking to a previous caller, the new call waits if an idle telephone line is available. If all N lines are occupied, the new call gets a busy signal and is cleared from the system.

Suppose calls arrive in a Poisson process at a mean rate of $\lambda = 10$ calls per hour. Suppose further that the dispatcher's service times are distributed exponentially, with a mean time of $(1/\mu) = 3$ minutes; so $\mu = 20$ calls per hour. It is desired to find the minimum number N of phone lines to ensure a probability of less than 1% that a new call gets a busy signal.

For $S = 1$, $\lambda = 10$, and $\mu = 20$, Eq. (6-32a) reduces to

$$P_n = (\lambda/\mu)^n P_0 = (\tfrac{1}{2})^n P_0, \quad \text{where} \quad P_0 = \Big[\sum_{n=0}^{N} P_n\Big]^{-1} = \Big[\sum_{n=0}^{N} (\tfrac{1}{2})^n\Big]^{-1}.$$

The equilibrium probability that a new call is cleared is $P_N = (\tfrac{1}{2})^n P_0 =$ probability that all N lines are occupied. Table 6-2 shows the necessary calculations for $N = 1, 2, \ldots, 7$. It is seen that $N = 6$ lines provide the

TABLE 6-2

Emergency Phone Service—Probability P_N That a Call Is Cleared from the System

Number of lines N	$P_0 = [\sum_{n=0}^{N} (\tfrac{1}{2})^n]^{-1}$	$P_N = (\tfrac{1}{2})^N P_0$
1	$(1 + \tfrac{1}{2})^{-1} \quad = \tfrac{2}{3}$	$(\tfrac{1}{2})(\tfrac{2}{3}) = 0.3333$
2	$(1 + \tfrac{1}{2} + \tfrac{1}{4})^{-1} = 4/7$	$(\tfrac{1}{4})(\tfrac{4}{7}) = 0.1428$
3	$8/15$	0.0667
4	$16/31$	0.0322
5	$32/63$	0.0158
6	$64/127$	0.0079
7	$128/255$	0.0039

minimum waiting room consistent with a "calls cleared" probability P_N of less than 0.01.

(c)   *Example 2: "No-Queue" Ambulance Service*

The limited waiting room model can be applied to systems where customers are cleared whenever all servers are busy. In this case, no one ever waits, and the term "no-queue system" is appropriate. For example, suppose Middletown provides ambulance service with S ambulances. When all ambulances are busy, a new ambulance customer does not wait for one to become idle. Instead, a taxicab is used to provide inferior substitute service. Therefore, the maximum number of customers in the real ambulance system is $N = S$. Supposing equilibrium, Poisson arrivals at a mean rate λ, and exponentially distributed service times with a mean time $1/\mu$, Eq. (6-32) becomes

$$P_n = (1/n!)(\lambda/\mu)^n P_0, \quad \text{where} \quad P_0 = [\sum_{n=0}^{S} (1/n!)(\lambda/\mu)^n]^{-1}.$$

The equilibrium probability that all the server ambulances are busy is given by

$$P_S = \frac{(1/S!)(\lambda/\mu)^n}{\sum_{n=0}^{S} (1/n!)(\lambda/\mu)^n} = \frac{a^S/S!}{\sum_{n=0}^{S} (a^n/n!)}, \tag{6-33}$$

where $a = (\lambda/\mu)$ is the mean traffic load offered to the ambulance system. Since a fraction P_S of this load is cleared without service, the mean load actually handled is $a(1 - P_S)$.

Equation (6-33) has been in use for more than half a century in the telephone industry, where it serves as a model to decide how many telephone trunks should connect two offices, based on the mean traffic load to be served. It is called the Erlang loss formula. Excellent charts, giving numerical values for $S \leq 80$, can be found in Reference [13].

6-7   Conclusion

On the supposition that the methodology may be novel to many readers, much of this chapter has been devoted to basic mathematical exposition rather than to illustrative models. Even so, consideration has been limited to systems in equilibrium with Poisson arrivals and exponentially distributed service times. Further, no material is offered on priorities, inventory problems, cyclic service, or multiple bottlenecks in series. For more complete discussions, at varying levels of sophistication, the reader is referred to standard texts on queueing theory by Cooper [6], Cox and Smith [7], Morse [14], Prabhu [16], and Saaty [17].

It is possible to make theoretical analyses of many service systems where the arrival or service distributions are different than those considered here. However, analysis easily can become exceedingly messy even where the appropriate methodology is known. Hence it is common to engage in computer simulation of complex real systems. Such simulation often can be checked out by applying them first to simple situations where analytical solutions are known. Further, it sometimes turns out that simple approximations yield adequate accuracy. For both these reasons, the theory can prove to be quite useful even in problems too complex for complete formal solution.

The earliest efforts to model congestion phenomena were occasioned by the need to design telephone networks to handle traffic economically while maintaining a reasonable quality of service. As a result of 70 years' work by numerous mathematicians and engineers, the present state of the art for communications systems modeling is at an awesome level of sophistication. The intrepid reader may explore it at great depth in a monumental work by Kleinrock [12]. In the present context, the main applications are the planning of municipal telephone services (Example 1 of Section 6.5) and of information retrieval systems. An example of the latter is the medical information center modeled by Dei Rossi [8].

Beginning in the 1950s, queueing theory was applied to the modeling and control of automobile traffic. The basic tools, therefore, are developed in an elementary manner by Ashton [1] and more thoroughly by Haight [10]. Recent work is exemplified by De Smit [9] on congestion at signalized intersections, by Blumenfeld and Weiss [3] on the merging of vehicles at expressway ramps, and by Morse and Jaffee [15] on interference between cars as they overtake each other.

Serious congestion problems often arise at the interfaces between two modes of travel. Such interfaces, often called terminals, are called upon to hold wildly fluctuating numbers of customers for short periods of time. Two interesting studies are by Kholi [11] on the modeling of seaport operations and by Browne *et al.* [4] on baggage claim systems at large international airports.

When patients must wait to enter a hospital or to receive service within it, they may suffer irreparable damage. Further, valuable resources can be wasted on skilled custodial services to patients waiting unduly long for diagnostic or medical procedures. Among others, Bithell [2] has considered the hospital admissions process, and Shonick [18] has modeled accumulations of patients within the hospital.

Among possible applications of queueing theory to classic municipal services, perhaps the most significant one is in the selection of locations and operational doctrines for fire-fighting companies. This important topic will be discussed at length in Chapter 7.

PROBLEMS

1. Give specific examples of queues with

    (a)   a single server,
    (b)   several servers,
    (c)   self-service,
    (d)   no waiting room,
    (e)   limited waiting room,
    (f)   effectively unlimited waiting room,
    (g)   first-come first-served queue discipline,
    (h)   priority queue discipline,
    (i)   random order of service,
    (j)   bulk service,
    (k)   service time which increases with queue size,
    (l)   service time which decreases with queue size,
    (m)   balking.

2. Middletown's Harbor Tunnel has a flow capacity of $\mu = 2000$ cars per hour. Commencing at 4 P.M. on weekdays, the following are the approximate mean arrival rates:

4:00–4:30 P.M.	1000 cars per hour
4:30–5:00 P.M.	2000 cars per hour
5:00–5:30 P.M.	3000 cars per hour
5:30–6:00 P.M.	2000 cars per hour
after 6:00 P.M.	1000 cars per hour

   (a) Estimate the mean queue size, as a function of time, caused by oversaturation.

   (b) Estimate the total delay to all vehicles, in units of vehicle-hours, caused by oversaturation.

   (*Answer:* 500 hours per afternoon.)

   (c) It is proposed to improve the tunnel's operation so μ will be increased by 10%. What is the resultant saving in total delay?

   (*Answer:* 37.5% or 188 hours per afternoon.)

3. Middletown's Board of Elections tries to maintain the following service standard at election booths: "During the busiest hour of the day, the voters' average waiting time should not exceed 10 minutes." It is observed that 2 minutes is the average time taken by one voter in the election booth.

   (a) Assuming Poisson arrivals and exponentially distributed service times, estimate the maximum number of persons to be served by a one-booth voting place during the busiest hour of the day.

   (*Answer:* 25.)

   (b) Repeat part (a) for a voting place with two booths serving a single queue of voters.

   (*Answer:* 54.)

   (c) In what way(s) are the assumptions of the model, used in parts (a) and (b), incorrect? Would a correct model predict larger or smaller results? Why?

4. There are two phone booths at City Hall. One is at the entrance, while the other is at the entrance of the men's room, out of sight and a 4-minute walk away. It is known that the average time for a phone call is 3 minutes and that each of the phones serves an average of 10 calls per hour. Suppose that you wish to make a call and go to one of these

phones. On arrival, you find that there is one person making a call and a second person already waiting ahead of you. Would you expect to get a phone sooner by walking to the other phone or by waiting where you are?

(*Answer:* Stay where you are.)

5. At Middletown's school dental clinic, patients are given appointments for 9 A.M., 10 A.M., 11 A.M.,..., 4 P.M. The time to serve a patient, by the one dentist in attendance, is drawn from an exponential distribution with a mean time of 10 minutes. It is desired to have a probability of at least 75% that the patients arriving at any one hour are served before the arrival of the next group of patients. What is the maximum number of appointments that should be made for any one hour?

(*Answer:* 4.)

6. Middletown's garbage trucks, when filled, go to the municipal incinerator to be emptied. The incinerator has a single unloading bay which, at present, takes a mean time of 10 minutes to serve one garbage truck. A new unloading system is under consideration. If adopted, the mean service time would be reduced to 5 minutes. The new system would incur added costs of $25 per hour. A garbage truck and crew cost $25 per hour. What is the minimum average rate of truck arrivals that would justify installation of the new system? Assume Poisson arrivals and exponentially distributed service times.

(*Answer:* 3.6 trucks per hour.)

7. A single-server system has waiting room limited to three customers; so the maximum number in the system is four. Service times are distributed exponentially with a mean time of 12 minutes. Customers arrive in a Poisson process at a mean rate of 10 per hour. Find equilibrium values for

(a) the probabilities of $n = 0, 1, 2, 3, 4$ customers in the system;
(b) the mean number of customers in the system;
(c) the probability that a newly arrived customer will have to wait for service;
(d) the probability that a newly arrived customer will be served without waiting;
(e) the probability that a newly arrived customer will be cleared without receiving service.

(*Answer:* (a) $P_0 = \frac{1}{31}$, etc.; (b) $\frac{98}{31}$; (c) $\frac{14}{31}$; (d) $\frac{1}{31}$; (e) $\frac{16}{31}$.)

8. There are three spaces at the taxi stand in front of the Hotel Metropolis. Taxis arrive in a Poisson process at a mean rate of 10 per hour. If a taxi finds an empty space, it waits for a passenger. If all three spaces are filled by waiting taxis, it goes away to look for business elsewhere. Potential taxi passengers arrive at a mean rate of 10 per hour. An arriving potential passenger takes a taxi if one or more taxis are waiting. If no taxi is waiting, the potential passenger goes away at once to Main Street, a block away, and hails a cruising taxi. What is the probability that a newly arrived potential passenger will engage his taxi at the Hotel Metropolis taxi stand?

    Hint   Let the passengers be the servers and the taxis be the customers.

    (*Answer:* $\frac{3}{4}$.)

REFERENCES

[1]   Ashton, W. D., *The Theory of Road Traffic Flow*. Wiley, New York, 1966.
[2]   Bithell, J. F., A class of discrete-time models for the study of hospital admissions. *Operations Research* 17, No. 1, 48–69 (1969).
[3]   Blumenfeld, D. E., and Weiss, G. H., Merging from an acceleration lane. *Transportation Science* 5, No. 2 161–168 (1971).
[4]   Browne, J., Kelley, J. and Le Bourgeois, P., Maximum inventories in baggage claim. *Transportation Science* 4, No. 1, 64–78 (1970).
[5]   Burke, P. J., quoted in Cooper [6, pp. 156–158]. Burke's heuristic proof appears to be unpublished.
[6]   Cooper, R. B., *Introduction to Queueing Theory*. Macmillan, New York, 1972.
[7]   Cox, D. R., and Smith, W. L., *Queues*. Methuen, London, 1961.
[8]   Dei Rossi, J. A., A telephone-access bio-medical information center. *Operations Research* 20, No. 3, 643–667 (1972).
[9]   De Smit, J. H. A., Transient behavior of the queue at a fixed cycle traffic light. *Transportation Research* 5, No. 1, 1–14 (1971).
[10] Haight, F. A., *Mathematical Theories of Traffic Flow*. Academic Press, New York, 1963.
[11] Kholi, U. K., Quantitative model to represent port operations. *Opsearch (India)* 5, No. 2, 75–87 (1968).
[12] Kleinrock, L., *Communications Nets*. McGraw-Hill, New York, 1965.
[13] Molina, E. C., *Poisson's Exponential Binomial Limit*. Van Nostrand-Reinhold, Princeton, New Jersey, 1942.
[14] Morse, P. M., *Queues, Inventory and Maintenance*. Wiley, New York, 1958.
[15] Morse, P. M., and Jaffee, H. J., A queueing model for car passing. *Transportation Science* 5, No. 1, 48–63 (1971).
[16] Prabhu, N. U., *Queues and Inventories*. Wiley, New York, 1965.
[17] Saaty, T. L., *Elements of Queueing Theory*. McGraw-Hill, New York, 1961.
[18] Shonick, W., A stochastic model for occupancy-related random variables in general-acute hospitals. *Journal of American Statistical Association* 65, No. 332, 1474–1500 (1970).

Chapter 7

Location of Public Facilities

This chapter considers methods for locating fire stations, clinics, roads, transit lines, and other fixed-location facilities for customers who are dispersed about the urban area. The main objective of analysis is to find sites that minimize travel times or costs which arise because the facilities are not located on their customers' premises. There are, of course, many other considerations that affect where a facility may be sited. These include political pressures, zoning restrictions, site purchase costs, and physical site deficiencies. These considerations are viewed as constraints which eliminate or make it very difficult to adopt some otherwise potentially valid locations.

7-1 A Single Facility

Suppose that one facility serves the entire area of interest. Suppose further that the "cost" of this service depends on the relative locations of the facility and of the customers it serves. Under these assumptions, the optimum facility location is the one that minimizes the sum of the location-dependent costs for all customers. Let

$c(x, y \mid x_0, y_0)$ = the location-dependent "cost" of one unit of service, provided to a customer at location (x, y), by the server located at (x_0, y_0). Most often, this "cost" is travel time or a function of travel time.

$w(x, y)\, dx\, dy$ = service "demand" by customers in the area of size $dx\, dy$, located between x and $(x + dx)$ and between y and $(y + dy)$. Thus, $w(x, y)$ is the service "demand" density function.

$C_T(x_0, y_0)$ = total location-dependent cost, given that the facility is located at (x_0, y_0).

The "demand" might be the number of service calls requested per unit time. In the case of fires, this number ought to be weighted to reflect anticipated losses as a function of the actual structures at risk in each location. On the basis of the above definitions, $C_T(x_0, y_0)$ is simply the weighted integral of $c(x, y \mid x_0, y_0)$, taken over the entire area to be served:

$$C_T(x_0, y_0) = \iint\limits_{\substack{\text{all } (v,y) \\ \text{within area}}} w(x, y) c(x, y \mid x_0, y_0)\, dx\, dy. \qquad (7\text{-}1)$$

The location problem is solved by finding x^* and y^* such that $C_T(x_0, y_0)$ is a minimum for $x_0 = x^*$ and $y_0 = y^*$. Formally, x^* and y^* are values of x_0 and y_0 that satisfy

$$\frac{\partial C_T(x_0, y_0)}{\partial x_0} = 0 \quad \text{and} \quad \frac{\partial C_T(x_0, y_0)}{\partial y_0} = 0. \qquad (7\text{-}2)$$

There are several possible functional forms for the location-dependent cost $c(x, y \mid x_0, y_0)$. The most obvious one is the distance between (x, y) and (x_0, y_0):

$$c(x, y \mid x_0, y_0) = c_0[(x - x_0)^2 + (y - y_0)^2]^{1/2}. \qquad (7\text{-}3)$$

Here, c_0 is the cost per unit distance. If travel time is to be the unit of cost, then c_0 is the inverse of the average velocity. If the study area is traversed by a rectangular street grid, aligned parallel to the x and y axes, a better measure would be

$$c(x, y \mid x_0, y_0) = c_0(\mid x - x_0 \mid + \mid y - y_0 \mid). \qquad (7\text{-}4)$$

It may be that the cost does not increase linearly with distance. For example, in evaluating the cost of reaching a school from home, one would find a discontinuity between distances deemed walkable and larger distances that require service by a school bus.

If $w(x, y) = w$, independent of location, and if $c(x, y \mid x_0, y_0)$ is a function only of distance between (x, y) and (x_0, y_0), then the values (x^*, y^*), which minimize Eq. (7-1), will be at the center of the area. However, even in this case, some analysis may be appropriate to find out how sensitive the total cost $C_T(x_0, y_0)$ is to small displacements from the optimum (x^*, y^*). It may well be that a fairly wide range of locations will result in rather negligible cost penalties.

For practical analysis, it may be appropriate to divide the study area into N zones and to approximate all locations, within any zone j, by one zone centroid (x_j, y_j). Then the integral equation (7-1) can be replaced by the sum

$$C_T(x_0, y_0) = \sum_{j=1}^{N} w_j c(x_j, y_j \mid x_0, y_0), \tag{7-5}$$

where w_j is the total "demand" from zone j.

7-2 Districting

When two or more facilities are to be located in an area, and each facility is to serve its own district, one faces the problem of delineating the district boundaries. Because the overall problem is very complicated, practical analysis is likely to take the form of an iterative procedure, wherein one alternates between

(1) a search for the best facility location within each district, given the district boundaries, and

(2) a search for the best district boundaries, given all of the facility locations.

There is no guarantee that this procedure will converge on an optimum solution. However, given a reasonably good starting solution, it should result in significant improvement toward a near-optimum configuration.

Step (1), above, consists of the repeated application, once for each district, of the single-facility location analysis developed in Section 7-1. For step (2), we exhibit a procedure, by Keeney [6], here simplified by the use of the assumptions that customer demands are distributed uniformly in the region and that the cost of serving a customer is directly proportional to the distance between him and the facility that serves him. The procedure can readily be modified to work even if these assumptions are relaxed.

Let the region be bounded by a given "external boundary." Let there be N given facility locations, designated by $F_j = (x_j, y_j)$ for $j = 1, 2, \ldots, N$. The problem is to divide the region into N districts, one about each facility, in such a way that any location is nearer to its own district's facility than to any other facility. The procedure is as follows:

1. Select the first facility, at F_1, to serve the entire region. For the region, thus spanned by $n = 1$ district, the optimal district boundary is merely the region's external boundary.

2. The entire region is now divided into n districts, with known optimal boundaries, centered on facilities at $F_1, F_2, \ldots, F_n$.

3. The one facility at F_{n+1} is added. The region is redivided optimally into $(n + 1)$ districts, centered on facilities at $F_1, F_2, \ldots, F_{n+1}$.

4. If $(n + 1) = N$, the procedure is finished. If not, replace the label $(n + 1)$ by the label n and go to step 2.

It remains only to describe a procedure for accomplishing step 3 above. This is most easily done by considering two examples, one without and one with an external boundary.

Suppose that there are $n = 3$ districts, optimally bounded as shown in Fig. 7-1. Each internal boundary, between two adjacent districts, is a locus of points equidistant from the two districts' facilities. A fourth facil-

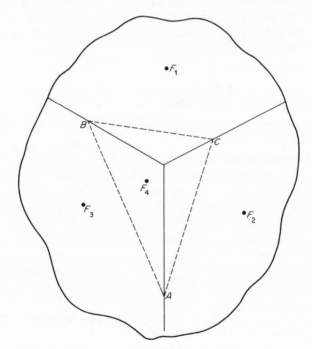

FIG. 7-1 Optimal Districting—The Addition of One District with Internal Boundaries Only

ity, at F_4, is added as shown. District 4 will consist of all points nearer to F_4 than to F_1, F_2, or F_3. Since F_4 lies in the old district 3, points in this district, nearer to F_4 than to F_3, will be reassigned to district 4. The line, within old district 3, equidistant from F_3 and F_4, is drawn from A to B. This is the new boundary between districts 3 and 4. Beyond point B, the new boundary lies between districts 1 and 4. Therefore, a line starting at B and equidistant from F_1 and F_4 is drawn across district 1 to point C. This is the new boundary between districts 1 and 4. Finally, a line equidistant from F_2 and F_4 is drawn from C to A across district 2. Thus, the boundaries of the new district, served by the facility at F_4, are developed

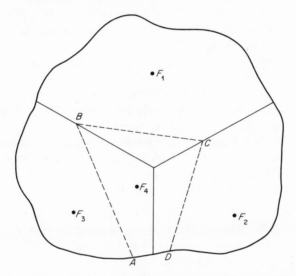

FIG. 7-2   Optimal Districting—The Addition of One District with Both Internal and External Boundaries

in a step-by-step manner. Within the new district, bounded by the dashed lines, the old district boundaries cease to exist. On the other hand, the addition of district 4 has not changed relative distances outside of this district. Therefore, old boundaries remain unchanged outside of the new district 4.

The procedure is almost unchanged if the external boundary becomes part of the new district's boundary. Figure 7-2 shows the previous illustration, now modified just enough to ensure that the external boundary will bound the new district 4. Following the previous argument, a new district 4 boundary is constructed from A to B to C. From C onward, the external boundary is the new district's boundary until point D is reached, where

D is equidistant from F_2 and F_4. The new district's boundary is completed by the line from D to A, equidistant from F_2 and F_4.

7-3   Location of Fire Stations

(a)   *The Problem*

The optimal deployment of fire stations is an appealing municipal service problem. Obviously, one major objective is to minimize the expected response time, measured from the moment of an alarm to the moment at which the fire is attacked by a suitable force. In aggregating response times, one should weight properly the values of lives and structures at risk in different locations. Then the first business of location analysis is to find the set of district boundaries and station locations, within the districts, that minimizes a properly weighted expected response time.

The relationship of a district to its fire company is as follows: When there is an alarm within the district, its own fire company responds unless it already is engaged in response to a prior alarm. A company in an adjacent district will respond only if the original district's company is already so engaged or if the fire is too large for one company.

Two levels of analysis will be considered:

1.   The first is the search for optimal district boundaries and station sites, based on the assumption that one may ignore fire company trips across district boundaries. Such a decoupling of districts is reasonable for those smaller, low-density cities, where it is a rare event to have two nearly simultaneous fires within one district.

2.   The second is the modification, in district boundaries and sites, that results from inclusion in the analysis of calls for companies to fight fires in districts other than their own. Such modifications are significant for large, high-density cities such as New York, where one district may have as many as 20 fire calls on its busier days.

In the following discussion, it will be assumed that the number of districts, each served by one company, is decided upon before the location analysis commences. This may be the correct approach in places where the fire-fighting budget and the presumed optimal size of one fire company are not really subject to modification. Where these parameters can be changed, one can simplify matters a great deal by finding optimal deployments separately for 1, 2, 3, ... companies and then comparing the resultant configurations on the bases of cost and fire-fighting effectiveness.

(b)   *Methodology for Decoupled Districts*

The model described here, by Santone and Berlin [8], was applied to East Lansing, Michigan, where it resulted in a recommendation for three districts and a specific delineation of their boundaries.

The study area is modeled by a link-node network, as described for traffic assignment in Section 5.5. The individual link travel time c_{ij}, along the one link directed from node i to node j, is taken to be the expected traversal time for a fire engine. Let $C_{ij}*$ be the expected travel time for a fire engine, along the *minimum-time* link-node route, from any given origin node i to any given destination node j. Such minimum travel times can be found by use of the minimum-cost tree-building algorithm in Section 5-5. Because the model structure is thus made identical to the one for traffic assignment, the cost of a fire station siting study is minimized for cities, such as East Lansing, which have already completed major transportation planning projects.

Suppose that the specific boundaries of a fire district have been selected. Let D_j be the "demand" for fire protection in the immediate vicinity of any node j within that district. If all the district's D_j's are known, the optimum location for the fire station is made the node i that minimizes the weighted total expected travel cost W_i, where

$$W_i = \sum_j C_{ij}*D_j. \qquad (7\text{-}6)$$

The sum is taken over all j's within the district. Given a reasonably efficient computer program, it is quite practical to evaluate W_i for every available i and thus find the best location by enumeration of all possibilities.

Let

$D_{k(j)}$ = protection "demand" for the kth structure in the neighborhood of node j,

$L_{k(j)}$ = expected loss from one fire in the kth structure at node j, and

$P_{k(j)}$ = probability that there is a fire, during any one year, in the kth structure at node j.

Then

$$D_j = \sum_k D_{k(j)} = \sum_k P_{k(j)}L_{k(j)},$$

where the summation is over all structures associated with node j. In a practical context, the estimates for $P_{k(j)}$ and $L_{k(j)}$ may have to be made subjectively, using judgments by senior fire department personnel, supplemented by available insurance underwriter statistics. However, if money and time permit, these quantities can be developed more rigorously. One may set

$$P_{k(j)} = \sum_r a_k X_{kr} \quad \text{and} \quad L_{k(j)} = \sum_r b_k X_{kr},$$

where the X_k's are structural parameters, such as age or type of construction, and inventory parameters, such as the number of people endangered or the value of the structure's contents. The a_k's and b_k's are coefficients fitted on the basis of past fire experience. Some of the coefficients may be zero. For example, the number of people endangered is not a significant predictor for the probability of a fire, even though it affects the expected loss when there is a fire.

A more complete analysis would make $L_{k(j)}$ a function also of the fire house location node i, since the expected loss increases with increasing response time. This was pointed out but was not included in the East Lansing study.

There remains the problem of setting fire district boundaries. Rather than going through the formidable exercise of doing this analytically, a partially subjective approach was used. A number of nodes in the study area were chosen as suitable candidates for station sites, based on land availability, adjacent land use, streets in the immediate vicinity, and other site criteria. Then the street network model was used to generate "isochrones" of equal travel time around each candidate node. These isochrones provided the means to calculate land areas reachable within 1, 2, 3,...minutes of these nodes. Then, given the total number of fire stations, a first round assignment was made subjectively for the station location nodes and for their district boundaries. In doing this, an effort was made to maximize the fraction of the total land located within isochrones of short travel time from the station nodes.

Given the first round district boundaries, the station location model was used to relocate the station nodes, if necessary, to minimize the expected cost W_i, as given by Eq. (7-6). Then the district lines were shifted subjectively to reduce imbalances in work loads among districts. This iteration, of subjective boundary shifting and analytical station siting, was repeated a few times. No attempt was made to achieve formal convergence to the state where further iteration would produce no change at all.

(c) *The Modeling of Interactions among Districts*

Where fire companies have fairly light work loads, there is not overly much need to balance work loads closely to achieve uniformity. In such situations, the boundary between two districts is likely to be near optimal if it is placed so as to equalize the response time to it from both districts' stations. Further, small likelihood of near simultaneous fires, within a district, makes it unnecessary to consider interdistrict calls. The situation is quite different where fire companies are busy a large fraction of the time. In such environments, one ought to include the interdistrict calls explicitly in the model formulation. Queueing theory, discussed in the previous chapter, is the obvious modeling tool for exhibiting the probabilities that such calls occur. We illustrate with an idealized two-district model, developed by the New York City Fire Project and reported by Blum [1].

Suppose a region R is to be served by two companies. One company serves a response district A, and the other company serves the remaining district B, where $B = R - A$. It is assumed that fires occur independently at random in time according to a Poisson process. Calls from district A are labeled as "type-A customer arrivals," with mean arrival rate $\lambda_A = \lambda(A)$. Calls from district B are labeled as "type-B customer arrivals," with mean rate $\lambda_B = \lambda(B) = \lambda(R) - \lambda(A)$. The service discipline is as follows:

1.   If a customer arrives when both servers are idle, it is served by its own district's server.

2.   If a customer arrives when its own district's server is busy and the other district's server is idle, it is served by the other district's server.

3.   If a customer arrives when both servers are busy, it is served from a location outside the system being considered.

For simplicity, it is assumed further that:

4.   Service times for all fires are drawn from an exponential distribution, with mean time $1/\mu$, independent of fire locations or the identities of the servers. This assumption may not be reasonable if the time spent traveling to a fire is a large fraction of the time spent actually fighting that fire.

5.   The system is in statistical equilibrium.

The effect of assumption 3 is to produce a system with no waiting room, somewhat like the example of Section 6-6(a). However, now one must label the state probabilities to show explicitly which of the servers is busy. Let

P_0 = probability that both servers are idle.

P_{1A} = probability that one customer is being served by district A's server and that the other server is idle.

P_{1B} = probability that one customer is being served by district B's server and that the other server is idle.

P_2 = probability that both servers are busy.

The equilibrium analysis can be made with an intuitive detailed balance argument similar to the one used for a single server in Section 6-3. Figure 7-3 shows the four possible states of the system, together with the mean transition rates among them. For example, the mean transition rate from state (0) to state (1A) is the arrival rate λ_A of customers in district A, multiplied by the probability P_0 that both servers are idle. Similarly, the mean transition rate from state (2) to state (1B) is the service completion rate μ of the server assigned to district A, multiplied by the probability P_2 that both servers are busy.

In equilibrium, the sum of the mean transition rates out of a state must equal the sum of the mean transition rates into it. Otherwise, the state probabilities would change with time. Hence

$$(\lambda_A + \lambda_B)P_0 = \mu(P_{1A} + P_{1B})$$

$$(\lambda_A + \lambda_B + \mu)P_{1A} = \lambda_A P_0 + \mu P_2$$

$$(\lambda_A + \lambda_B + \mu)P_{1B} = \lambda_B P_0 + \mu P_2$$

$$2\mu P_2 = (\lambda_A + \lambda_B)(P_{1A} + P_{1B}).$$

Further, the sum of the state probabilities must be one:

$$P_0 + P_{1A} + P_{1B} + P_2 = 1.$$

The solution to these equations is

$$P_0 = \left[\frac{1}{1 + \rho + \rho^2/2}\right], \qquad P_{1A} = \left[\frac{\rho_A + \rho^2/2}{1 + \rho}\right]P_0$$

$$P_{1B} = \left[\frac{\rho_B + \rho^2/2}{1 + \rho}\right]P_0, \qquad P_2 = \left[\frac{\rho^2}{2}\right]P_0 \qquad (7\text{-}7)$$

Here $\rho = (\lambda_A + \lambda_B)/\mu$, $\rho_A = \lambda_A/\mu$, and $\rho_B = \lambda_B/\mu$.

The work load W of a fire company is defined as the equilibrium probability that it is busy serving a call. For the company serving district A, $W_A = P_{1A} + P_2$, and for the company serving district B, $W_B = P_{1B} + P_2$. The difference in work loads is found from Eqs. (7-7) to be

$$\Delta W = |W_A - W_B| = \left[\frac{|\rho_A - \rho_B|}{1 + \rho}\right]P_0. \qquad (7\text{-}8)$$

One must average four situations to obtain the overall mean call response time:

1. District A company responding to district A calls: Let T_{AA} be the mean response time for these. The mean rate of such calls is $(\lambda_A P_0 + \lambda_A P_{1B})$.

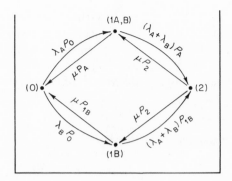

FIG. 7-3   Transition Diagram for Two Fire Companies

2.   District A company responding to district B calls: Let T_{AB} be the mean response time for these. The mean rate of such calls is $\lambda_B P_{1B}$.

3.   District B company responding to district B calls: Let T_{BB} be the mean response time for these. The mean rate of such calls is $(\lambda_B P_0 + \lambda_B P_{1A})$.

4.   District B company responding to district A calls: Let T_{BA} be the mean response time for these. The mean rate of such calls is $\lambda_A P_{1A}$.

The overall rate of calls, actually served by the two companies, is the total call rate $\lambda_A + \lambda_B$, multiplied by the probability $(1 - P_2)$ that a call will be served from within the district. Thus, the mean call response time is

$$E(T) = \frac{\lambda_A(P_0 + P_{1B})T_{AA} + \lambda_B P_{1B} T_{AB} + \lambda_B(P_0 + P_{1A})T_{BB} + \lambda_A P_{1A} T_{BA}}{(\lambda_A + \lambda_B)(1 - P_2)}.$$

$$(7\text{-}9)$$

The effects of moving the boundary between two districts, on both work load balance and call response time, can now be studied in detail. As the boundary is moved, the arrival rates (λ_A, λ_B) and the mean response times $(T_{AA}, T_{AB}, T_{BB}, T_{BA})$ will change, resulting in changing values for ΔW and $E(T)$, as found from Eqs. (7-8) and (7-9).

Problem 3, at the end of this chapter, considers the complementary question of optimal station location, given fixed district boundaries.

(d)   Further Work

Much research has been done on the problems of locating fire stations and other emergency units, such as ambulances and police patrol cars. The physical location analysis, introduced here, has been extended and supplemented by logistics analysis to find the best tactics for overloaded systems. For example, there is the problem of where and when some fire companies should temporarily relocate at times of exceptionally heavy and uneven demand. Chaiken and Larson [3] offer a review of such problems, together with a comprehensive bibliography of recent work.

7-4   Optimal Transportation Routing

The problem of finding the optimal route for a road or transit line, between given origin and destination points, is quite complicated. One ought to consider the following:

1.   Direct costs, to builder and operator, of land, construction, and maintenance. The maintenance costs, and perhaps the others, depend on the traffic volume diverted to the route.

2.   Direct benefits to those travelers who will use the route. These travelers include persons diverted from other roads and persons who will make trips they did not find worth making in the absence of the new facility.

3.   Indirect costs including the losses faced by those who must relocate and by those who must continue life next to the new route. Also there is the resource cost to society of the new traffic generated by the route.

4.   Indirect benefits including the gains by those who can profitably exploit locations next to the new route, by travelers elsewhere who benefit from traffic diversion, and by the greater society through the route's indirect contribution to the economy.

The situation is so complex that today there is no practical alternative to the proposing of a modest number of specific alternative routes, followed by an economic analysis of each one, and concluding with a partially subjective choice of which among them is best. Clearly, such an approach may fail to consider routes that are better than any of those actually analyzed.

There has been some research on finding an optimum route by search techniques which consider all location possibilities. We illustrate with a model, adapted from a paper by Friedrich [5], which seeks only to minimize the direct costs of land, construction, and maintenance. Despite great mathematical sophistication, the Friedrich model is really rather primitive and can be viewed as no more than a precursor to as yet nonexistent practical routing formalisms.

At this point, an apology is in order regarding the complexity of the next few paragraphs. The reader might be entirely justified if he timidly

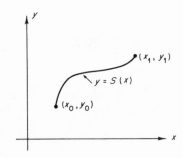

FIG. 7-4   The Optimum Route Problem

skips forward to the next section. However, it is hoped that he will persist and thus capture at least some of the flavor of Friedrich's valuable contribution.

Formally, the problem is to find the cheapest route between two points, (x_0, y_0) and (x_1, y_1), on the plane which models the region under consideration. Let any route, between the two points, be labeled by the general function $y = S(x)$, as shown in Fig. 7-4. The following information is assumed to exist for all locations along any feasible route $y = S(x)$:

1.   The purchase cost of a unit length of land for the route's right of way: Let $a_1[x, S(x)]$ be this cost, expressed in terms of annual rent, at any route point $[x, S(x)]$.

2.   The construction cost of a unit length of route: Let this cost be $a_2[x, S(x)]$, expressed in terms of annual rent, at any route point $[x, S(x)]$.

3.   The annual traffic-independent cost of maintaining a unit length of route: Let $a_3[x, S(x)]$ be this cost at any route point $[x, S(x)]$.

4.   The annual volume of traffic joining the route at any unit length thereof: Let this be $q[x, S(x)]$ at the route point $[x, S(x)]$. The unit of traffic is a vehicle, for roads, or a passenger, for transit. The annual volume is the number of units per year.

5.   The traffic-dependent maintenance and operating costs resulting from one traffic unit's use of the route: These costs depend on how far the unit travels and so are functions of where it enters and where it leaves the route. For simplicity, it is assumed possible to estimate these costs adequately on the basis of entering location alone. If so, one may set $w[x, S(x)]$ as the cost of traffic-dependent maintenance and operation for one traffic unit entering the route at $[x, S(x)]$.

On the assumption that all direct road costs can be expressed in the functional forms just defined, one can formally express the total annual cost $R(S)$ of any particular route $S(x)$ between (x_0, y_0) and (x_1, y_1). The total annual cost $r[x, S(x)]$ of a unit length of route at $[x, S(x)]$ is the sum of the costs discussed above:

$$r[x, S(x)] = a_1[x, S(x)] + a_2[x, S(x)] + a_3[x, S(x)]$$
$$+ q[x, S(x)]w[x, S(x)]. \quad (7\text{-}10)$$

Consider now an infinitesimal segment of the route, starting at $[x, S(x)]$ and ending at $[x + dx, S(x) + dS(x)]$. The length of this segment is

$$\{(dx)^2 + [dS(x)]^2\}^{1/2} = \left\{1 + \left[\frac{dS(x)}{dx}\right]^2\right\}^{1/2} dx. \quad (7\text{-}11)$$

The annual cost of the infinitesimal road segment is the product of Eqs. (7-10) and (7-11). The total annual cost $R(S)$ of the route $S(x)$ is the integral of this product, evaluated from x_0 to x_1:

$$R(S) = \int_{x_0}^{x_1} r[x, S(x)] \left\{1 + \left[\frac{dS(x)}{dx}\right]^2\right\}^{1/2} dx. \quad (7\text{-}12)$$

The problem is to find that function $S(x)$ that minimizes $R(S)$. Let $F = F[x, S(x), dS(x)/dx]$ be the symbol for the entire product function to be integrated as per Eq. (7-12). Then Eq. (7-12) can be written succinctly as

$$R(S) = \int_{x_0}^{x_1} F\left[\frac{x, S(x), dS(x)}{dx}\right] dx. \quad (7\text{-}13)$$

It is shown, in the calculus of variations, that the function $S(x)$ that minimizes the $R(S)$ in Eq. (7-13) is the $S(x)$ that satisfies the Euler–Lagrange differential equation,

$$\frac{\partial F}{\partial S} - \frac{d}{dx}\left[\frac{\partial F}{\partial(dS/dx)}\right] = 0, \quad (7\text{-}14)$$

where $F = F[x, S(x), dS(x)/dx]$ from Eq. (7-13). The problem of finding the minimum-cost route thus is reduced to solving the differential equation (7-14), subject to the boundary conditions $S(x_0) = y_0$ and $S(x_1) = y_1$.

To illustrate this model in the simplest possible way, it will now be used to demonstrate the self-evident proposition that the shortest route between two points is a straight line. Suppose that land, construction, maintenance, and traffic-dependent costs are all independent of location. Then $r[x, S(x)] = r$, a constant, and

$$F = r\left[1 + \left(\frac{dS}{dx}\right)^2\right]^{1/2}.$$

Taking derivatives, one finds $\partial F / \partial S = 0$ and

$$\frac{d}{dx}\left[\frac{\partial F}{\partial (dS/dx)}\right] = \frac{r(d^2S/dx^2)}{[1 + (dS/dx)^2]^{3/2}} \ ;$$

so the Euler–Lagrange equation (7-14) becomes

$$\frac{-r(d^2S/dx^2)}{[1 + (dS/dx)^2]^{3/2}} = 0. \tag{7-15}$$

The denominator of Eq. (7-15) is always greater than 1. Therefore, $(d^2S/dx^2) = 0$ and so

$$S(x) = c_0 + c_1 x. \tag{7-16}$$

The constants of integration, c_0 and c_1, must be chosen so that $S(x_0) = y_0$ and $S(x_1) = y_1$. Thus, as expected, $S(x)$ turns out to be a straight line from the given origin to the given destination.

The Friedrich methodology can, of course, be applied to far less trivial cases than this example. However, the mathematics is then likely to be awkward for anything other than a numerical solution of the pertinent Euler–Lagrange equation.

7-5 Location of Transit Stations along a Given Route

Once a transit route is decided, it remains to find the spacing of stations that minimizes the total travel time of passengers between their origins and their destinations. This problem was considered by Vuchic and Newell [9] for the important special case in which the travelers all commute to one central terminal. The parameters included were passenger distribution along the line, access speed, dynamic characteristics of the train, standing times of trains in stations, and the passengers' transfer times at the stations.

Rather than reproduce the quite complicated Vuchic–Newell model, we exhibit here an idealized version with just enough internal structure to make possible a demonstration of an appropriate solution methodology. The procedure will be to find the optimum station spacing, given the number n of stations to be used by boarding passengers. Thereafter, total passenger travel times can be compared, for the possible values of n, to decide on the optimum number of stations. The simplified model, Fig. 7-5,

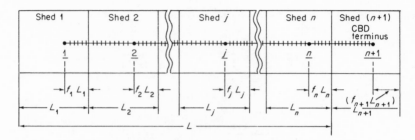

FIG. 7-5   Diagram of Model for Location of Transit Stations

embodies the following assumptions and definitions:

1.   The transit line consists of a straight route, starting at station 1 and ending at the central terminus, station $(n + 1)$. Figure 7-5 shows each station's "shed," defined as the area whose residents will use the station. The people residing in shed $(n + 1)$ are so near to the terminus that they do not use the train at all. Let L_j be the length of station shed j. Let $L = \sum_{j=1}^{n} L_j$ be the given length of the area whose residents ride the transit line. To simplify the derivation, the analysis will not be extended to find the length L_{n+1} of the terminal's shed.

2.   Station j is located at a distance $f_j L_j$ from the downtown boundary of station shed j.

3.   Trains travel at a constant speed v between stations. The time loss, due to acceleration and deceleration at any station, is lumped with the time the train stands still at that station. Let T_0 be this composite station dwell time.

4.   Passengers are distributed uniformly along the route, with a density of p passengers per unit length of route. Each passenger goes to the station that minimizes his total travel time from home to the terminus at station $(n + 1)$. Thus, the boundary between two station sheds is that line along which residents experience the same home–terminus travel times via either station.

5.   In traveling from home to station, passengers move along a rectangular street grid, aligned parallel to the transit line. With this assumption, the portions of their trips, perpendicular to the line, are independent of station location and need not be considered. Let v_a be the mean speed for that portion of a passenger's home–station trip which is parallel to the line.

6.   All passengers face the same delay distribution in effecting the transfer from access travel mode to the transit line. Thus, these delays can be ignored.

7.   The train is faster than the speed of travel to the station; so $v > v_a$.

On the basis of this model structure, the optimum station locations result from those values of L_j and f_j, where $j = 1, 2, \ldots, n$, that minimize the sum T of all the passengers' travel times, subject to the condition that $\sum_{j=1}^{n} L_j = L$, where L is the length of the served area.

By assumption 4, passengers are distributed uniformly along the transit line, with density p; so the number of passengers within station j's shed is pL_j. By assumption 5, one need consider only that portion of the home–station trip that is parallel to the transit line. Hence, of passengers originating in station shed j, a fraction f_j go an average distance $f_j L_j/2$, and the remaining fraction $(1 - f_j)$ go an average distance $(1 - f_j)L_j/2$. Thus, the total time spent by shed j passengers in traveling parallel to the line at a mean speed v_a is

$$T_j^{(1)} = \left\{ \frac{f_j[f_j L_j/2]}{v_a} + \frac{(1 - f_j)[(1 - f_j)L_j/2]}{v_a} \right\} \cdot (pL_j)$$

$$= \frac{p}{2v_a} (1 - 2f_j + 2f_j^2) L_j^2. \tag{7-17}$$

Once on the train, passengers who boarded at station j go a distance

$$f_j L_j + (L_{j+1} + L_{j+2} + \cdots + L_n) + (1 - f_{n+1})L_{n+1}$$

on the train which, when moving, is assumed to go at an average speed v. Since all passengers using the train are on board when the train leaves station n, they all experience the last leg, of length $(1 - f_{n+1})L_{n+1}$. Therefore, this term will be dropped as not affecting the relative locations of stations $1, 2, \ldots, n$. Based on this argument, the average time spent at train speed v by those boarding at station j is

$$(1/v)\left(f_j L_j + \sum_{i=j+1}^{n} L_i\right),$$

where it is to be understood that the sum term is zero for $j = n$.

Between station j and the terminus, there are $(n - j)$ intermediate stops, each contributing a delay T_0. Thus, the total time spent on the train by the pL_j passengers boarding at station j is

$$T_j^{(2)} = \left[(1/v)\left(f_j L_j + \sum_{i=j+1}^{n} L_i\right) + (n - j)T_0 \right](pL_j). \tag{7-18}$$

The sum T of all passengers' travel times, excluding some portions not dependent on station location, is thus

$$T = \sum_{j=1}^{n} (T_j{}^{(1)} + T_j{}^{(2)})$$

$$= p \sum_{j=1}^{n} \left[(n - j) T_0 L_j + \left(\frac{1 - 2f_j + 2f_j{}^2}{2v_a} + \frac{f_j}{v} \right) L_j{}^2 + \frac{1}{v} \sum_{i=j+1}^{n} L_i L_j \right].$$

$$(7\text{-}19)$$

One seeks values of f_k and L_k, for $k = 1, 2, \ldots, n$, that minimize T, subject to the constraint

$$(L - \sum_{j=1}^{n} L_j) = 0. \qquad (7\text{-}20)$$

The Lagrange multiplier methodology is appropriate for this. One sets

$$Z = T + \lambda(L - \sum_{j=1}^{n} L_j), \qquad (7\text{-}21)$$

where T is given by Eq. (7-19). If one then minimizes Z with respect to f_k, L_k, and λ, one obtains values of f_k and L_k that minimize T subject to Eq. (7-20). To minimize Z, one solves the $(2n + 1)$ simultaneous equations,

$$\frac{\partial Z}{\partial f_k} = 0, \qquad \frac{\partial Z}{\partial L_k} = 0, \qquad \text{and} \qquad \frac{\partial Z}{\partial \lambda} = 0,$$

for f_k, L_k, and λ.

Consider first $\partial Z/\partial f_k = 0$. One finds

$$\frac{\partial Z}{\partial f_k} = p \left[\frac{-2 + 4f_k}{2v_a} + \frac{1}{v} \right] L_k{}^2 = 0;$$

so

$$f_k = \tfrac{1}{2}(1 - v_a/v) \equiv f. \qquad (7\text{-}22)$$

Equation (7-22) shows that f_k is independent of k. Therefore, the subscript will be dropped in subsequent formulas, wherein f always will be defined by Eq. (7-22).

Now consider $\partial Z/\partial L_k = 0$. One finds

$$\frac{\partial Z}{\partial L_k} = p\left\{(n-k)T_0 + \left[\frac{1-2f+2f^2}{2v_a} + \frac{f}{v}\right](2L_k)\right.$$

$$\left. + \frac{1}{v}(L_1 + L_2 + \cdots + L_{k-1} + L_{k+1} + \cdots + L_n)\right\} + \lambda = 0.$$

By Eq. (7-20), $(L_1 + \cdots + L_{k-1} + L_k + \cdots + L_n) = L - L_k$. When one makes this substitution and solves for L_k, one finds

$$L_k = \left[\frac{\frac{\lambda}{p} + nT_0 + \frac{L}{v}}{\frac{1-2f+2f^2}{v_a} + \frac{2f}{v} - \frac{1}{v}}\right] + \left[\frac{T_0}{\frac{1-2f+2f^2}{v_a} + \frac{2f}{v} - \frac{1}{v}}\right]k.$$

The first of the two bracketed terms is independent of k and consists entirely of various parameters and the yet unevaluated λ. Thus, this term is a constant which, because of λ, remains to be evaluated. Call it λ^*. By use of Eq. (7-22), the second bracketed term can be much simplified to the result shown here:

$$L_k = \lambda^* + [v_a T_0/2f(1-f)]k. \tag{7-23}$$

By assumption 7, $v_a < v$; so $0 < f < 1$, and the coefficient of k in Eq. (7-23) is always positive. Therefore, the station shed lengths form an arithmetic progression, wherein shed k is longer than shed $(k-1)$ by an amount equal to the coefficient of k in Eq. (7-23). This result could have been anticipated, qualitatively, by noting that, with increasing k, there is an increase in the number of people on the train who are delayed by a station stop. Thus, the stations should be farther apart as the train approaches the terminus.

It remains to find λ^* by solving $\partial Z/\partial \lambda = 0$:

$$\partial Z/\partial \lambda = L - \sum_{j=1}^{n} L_j = 0.$$

If one substitutes for L_j from Eq. (7-23) and solves for λ^*, one finds

$$\lambda^* = L/n - [v_aT_0/2f(1-f)]^{\frac{1}{2}}(n+1),$$

so the final result is

$$L_k = L/n + [v_aT_0/2f(1-f)]^{\frac{1}{2}}(2k-n-1), \qquad (7\text{-}24)$$

with f as defined in Eq. (7-22).

Equation (7-24) gives the optimal station shed sizes for a given number of stations. The corresponding optimal spacing S_k, between stations k and $(k+1)$, is

$$S_k = fL_k + (1-f)L_{k+1}, \qquad (7\text{-}25)$$

as can be seen by inspection of Fig. 7-5. The optimum number of stations, n_{opt}, can be found by evaluating the optimal L_k's, for each value of n, and then comparing the consequent total travel times as given by Eq. (7-19). One can also find n_{opt} analytically. This was done by Vuchic and Newell [9], who offer the following approximation:

$$n_{\text{opt}} \cong I\{f - \tfrac{1}{2} + [4f(1-f)L/v_aT_0]^{1/2}\}. \qquad (7\text{-}26)$$

Here, $I\{\#\}$ is the largest integer less than or equal to the number $\{\#\}$ within the braces.

7-6   Conclusion

This chapter should have demonstrated that it is entirely possible to apply rational principles in siting public services. However, one should not be overly optimistic about how good the results will be. Superb sites, based on the observed world, can quickly become second rate if and when the population distribution or its life style changes. Contrariwise, poor site choices may work out quite well because the world will adjust to exploit them as they are. For example, residences and businesses are likely to locate in the neighborhood of a new road, or transit line, which originally was sited far away from potential users.

Even in the short run, the benefits of a service may not be very sensitive to the particular locations chosen for it. For example, Larson and Stephenson [7] have shown that the mean travel time, resulting from a totally random distribution of facilities, is reduced only 25% when the facilities are distributed optimally. So it seems that the analyst should be most cautious in defending any particular site plan, unless he has developed quite robust evidence that the alternatives are really inferior.

PROBLEMS

1. Fill in the steps leading to Eqs. (7-8) and (7-9).

2. Suppose that a land rectangle, of length L and width W, is divided into two equal-size rectangular fire districts, each one of length $L/2$ and width W. Suppose further that fires are equally likely throughout the area and that the total area fire call rate is λ. The two fire companies, one in each district, respond to calls by traveling at a mean speed v on a rectangular street grid oriented to be parallel to the district boundaries. Use the assumptions and the methodology of Section 7-3(b) to estimate, as a function of λ, the station locations that yield minimum average response times.

3. Develop a numerical illustration of the Vuchic–Newell model, Section 7-5. Assume a rail line about 25 miles long, with commuters traveling to stations at typical suburban street automobile speeds, and with fairly realistic operating characteristics for the train.

4. A high-density rapid transit line has four tracks; so it can offer both express (some stations) and local (all stations) service in both directions. Outline a model suitable for exploring the question of how to space the express stops where transfers can be made between the two services.

REFERENCES

[1] Blum, E. H., The New York City fire project. In *Analysis of Public Systems* (A. Drake, R. L. Keeney, and P. M. Morse, eds.), pp. 94–132. MIT Press, Cambridge, Massachusetts, 1972; see also Carter *et al.* [2].
[2] Carter, G. M., Chaiken, J. M., and Ignall, E., Response area for two emergency units. *Operations Research* **20**, No. 3, 571–594 (1972).
[3] Chaiken, J. M., and Larson, R. C. Methods for allocating urban emergency units. In *Analysis of Public Systems* (A. Drake, R. L. Keeney, and P. M. Morse, eds.), pp. 181–215. MIT Press, Cambridge, Massachusetts, 1972.

[4] Drake, A. Keeney, R. L., and Morse, P. M., ed., *Analysis of Public Systems.* MIT Press, Cambridge, Massachusetts, 1972.

[5] Friedrich, K., See Kahan, B. C., Precis of "The Calculus of Variations as a Method for Town and Country Planning." Res. Note RN/4087/BCK. Road Res. Lab., Harmondsworth, England, 1961.

[6] Keeney, R. L., A method for districting among facilities. *Operations Research* **20,** No. 3, 613–618 (1972).

[7] Larson, R. C., and Stevenson, K. A., Urban Redistricting and facility location. *Operations Research* **20,** No. 3, 595–612 (1972).

[8] Santone, L. C., and Berlin, G., Location of fire stations. In *Systems Analysis for Social Problems* (A. Blumstein, M. Kamrass, and A. B. Weiss, eds.), pp. 80–91. Washington Operations Res. Council (WORC), Washington, D.C., 1970.

[9] Vuchic, V. R., and Newell, G. F., Rapid transit interstation spacings. *Transportation Science* **2,** No. 4, 330–339 (1968).

Chapter *8*

Allocation of Public Resources

The first three sections of this chapter outline a theoretical framework for allocating resources so as to maximize the benefits received from their expenditure. Often, this theory is difficult to apply to public service systems because there is no immediately obvious way to evaluate, measure, or even visualize qualitatively the benefits to be obtained from alternative allocations. Hence the remainder of the chapter is devoted to some examples of how this problem has been approached in recent analyses of significant public activities.

8-1 The Benefit–Cost Viewpoint

In the following discussion, the word "good" will be used to describe any entity desired by an individual, group, company, or society. While some goods doubtlessly are free, or nearly so, we shall consider only goods sufficiently expensive, in money or other terms, so that the consumer will try to be efficient in his purchases. When a rational consumer faces a choice among two or more goods, all suitable for achieving some or all of the same desired objective, he will try to select the "best" one among them. How should he do this?

If each competing good can be fully characterized by its money cost, and if all goods offer the same benefits, then obviously the consumer should choose the cheapest one. Similarly, if the benefits of each good can be fully measured by a single quantity, such as money, and if all goods cost the same, then the highest-benefit good is best.

Suppose now that the goods have different costs and different benefits, but that all costs and benefits can be measured in terms of a common unit, such as money. One may then calculate, for each good, the ratio of benefits to costs. If the costs of all goods are acceptable, then the one with the largest benefit–cost ratio is the rational best choice. This ratio may still be the appropriate decision function even where the appropriate benefit measure is different from that for costs.

Example A tennis player may be offered a choice between two plans for court time at a neighborhood club. Plan A offers 100 hours for $200 and plan B offers 50 hours for $150. Clearly, plan A, at $\frac{1}{2}$ hour per dollar, offers a greater benefit–cost ratio than does plan B at $\frac{1}{3}$ hour per dollar. Note that the consumer may still have cause to prefer plan B.

It may be that a good can be purchased in varying amounts and that the benefit–cost ratio for it varies with the amount bought. If so, the best consumer choice may be a combination of different goods.

Example Middletown wishes to allocate efficiently its budget for lifeguards between two beaches, A and B. Table 8-1 shows costs and expected benefits, in lives saved per season, for various numbers of guards at both beaches. These figures have been obtained by tabulating the disasters of past years. Table 8-1 also shows the resultant benefit–cost ratios (BCRs)

TABLE 8-1
Data for Benefit–Cost Ratio (BCR) Example

Beach	Number of guards	Cost	Expected number of lives saved	BCR in lives per $10,000	Incremental BCR for one more guard in lives per $10,000
A	0	0	0	0	10.0
	1	$1000	1.00	10.0	5.5
	2	$2000	1.50	7.5	1.0
	3	$3000	1.60	5.3	0.5
	4	$4000	1.65	4.1	—
B	0	0	0	0	8.0
	1	$1000	0.80	8.0	4.0
	2	$2000	1.20	6.0	0.4
	3	$3000	1.24	4.2	0.2
	4	$4000	1.26	3.2	—

and the incremental BCRs for each additional guard. In this situation, where the BCRs change with the cost level, the choice of goods (i.e., guards at A or guards at B) should be made incrementally, one unit at a time, until the desired resource commitment is reached. At each step, the allocation should be to the good yielding the higher incremental BCR. Thus, the first guard should be at A, the second at B, the third at A, the fourth at B, and both the fifth and the sixth at A.

Evidently, if all resources are obtainable without limit at known money costs, and if all the desired goods can be quantified by a common measure, then there is no theoretical difficulty in allocating resources so as to maximize the aggregate value of the goods received. However, in attempting a real-world allocation, one often faces two vexing problems, one common to most purchasers and the second unique to governments, or equivalent agencies, which seek to allocate optimally for the public's benefit:

1. Resources may be limited; their costs may not all be quantifiable in money terms; and the alternative goods may not be commensurable.

2. A single purchaser should be satisfied by a simple maximization of the goods he obtains. But government is also much concerned with how the goods are distributed among the population.

8-2 The Allocation of Incommensurable Resources for Incommensurable Goods

One cannot expect to simultaneously maximize or minimize two or more independent variables of any one optimization problem. It is for this reason that it is exceedingly desirable to convert all costs for resources and benefits from goods into common money terms. But this is not always possible. Where it cannot be done, the usual practical approach is to maximize or minimize one variable, subject to specified constraints on the other variables. Some examples are as follows:

1. A bridge should be as strong as possible and as cheap as possible. The usual procedure is to devise a construction code to set minimum acceptable strength standards. One then builds the cheapest bridge that satisfies the constraints imposed by the code.

2. A town wishes to build public housing units. There are two scarce resources, building land and construction money. For spatial and political reasons, these resources are not readily interchangeable. There are two goods to be produced, a maximum number of housing units and a maximum

of amenity within each unit. The preferred procedure is likely to be the minimization of construction costs per housing unit, subject to constraints limiting the ranges of the other variables. Land will be conserved by setting a minimal amenity standard for the space per housing unit. Similarly, a minimum structural amenity standard will be determined by a building code enhanced by the social judgment of those in charge of the project. Thus, the cheapest acceptable houses would be built in as crowded a manner as possible up to the limit of the available construction money.

3.   Police manpower is to be allocated between traffic management and all other activities. Because traffic management, mainly at busy intersections and school crossings, is clearly understood, it is possible to set up meaningful standards for this activity. The other activities, mostly concerned with the fighting of crime, are more mysterious. Hence an arbitrary, but understandable, standard will be set for the manpower assigned to traffic. The remaining policemen will be assigned to the other activities.

4.   A municipally owned tract of land is to be developed into an industrial park. The incumbent administration proposes to allocate the land, among possible industries, by maximizing anticipated employment, subject to specified constraints on water supply, electric power, transportation facilities, and environmental fallout. The opposing party, now out of power, claims that this approach will favor declining, low-wage industry. It, therefore, proposes the alternative of maximizing output, in dollar terms, of the new industries, subject to the same constraints listed above.

These examples show that, while an arbitrary constraint methodology is indeed practical, a better approach is badly needed for the effective allocation of incommensurable variables for incommensurable goods. To this end, economists have devised a fairly sophisticated optimal resource allocation formalism, wherein "consumption indifference curves" are developed to group, in a measurable manner, the benefits conferred by combinations of incommensurable goods. This formalism, now to be outlined briefly, is developed further in standard texts, such as those by Baumol [1] or by Henderson and Quandt [8].

The approach is shown most easily by limiting oneself to two resources, A and B, which can be expended to obtain two desired goods, X and Y. For example, the resources might be land and money, and the goods might be public golf courses and ball fields.

Consider first the good X. It is assumed that, in return for any specified expenditure of resources A and B, one obtains a corresponding unique amount of good X. It is assumed further that any increase in expenditure, of either A or B, will result in an increase—or at worst no decrease—in the amount of good X. Given that these assumptions hold, one can plot, for

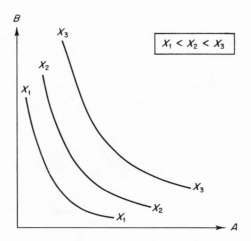

FIG. 8-1   Family of Production Indifference Curves

any given quantity of the good X, the relationship between expenditure of A and expenditure of B to achieve that quantity of X. Figure 8-1 shows a family of such relationships for various amounts of good X. It is a consequence of the assumptions that the curves of X, as functions of A and B, are convex with respect to the origin and that they do not cross one another. These curves are called "production indifference curves" because they were first used to consider the relationship between production inputs and resultant product, rather than the present resources and resultant good.

A similar family of production indifference curves can be drawn to show the quantity of good Y as a function of resource quantities A and B.

Now suppose that resources A and B are limited to amounts A_T and B_T and that these resources are to be used up entirely to purchase goods X and Y. Figure 8-2 shows the production indifference curves for good X, much as does Fig. 8-1, except that the range of resource values is bounded by A_T and B_T. The distances along axes A_X and B_X give the amounts of resources allocated to good X. The figure also shows production indifference curves for good Y, turned around so as to originate in the upper right corner of the diagram. The distances along axes A_Y and B_Y give the amounts of resources allocated to good Y. By this arrangement, every point on the graph shows an allocation of resources A and B to goods X and Y.

Consider the point P in Fig. 8-2. The distance from P down to the A_X axis is the amount of resource B allocated to good X. The remainder of the total B_T, from P up to the A_Y axis, is allocated to Y. Resource A is split similarly between goods X and Y. The production curve X_2, passing through

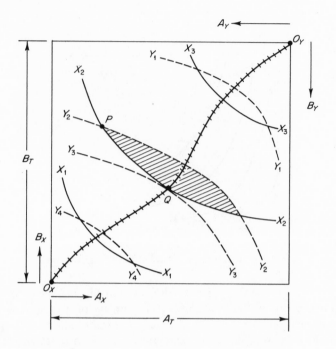

FIG. 8-2   Optimum Allocation Possibility Function

———: production indifference curve for good X; – – –: production indifference curve for good Y; +—+—+: optimum allocation possibility function.

P, shows the amount of X obtained with this allocation. The production curve Y_2 similarly shows the amount of Y. It can be seen now that P is not an optimum allocation point. The entire shaded region, bounded by X_2 and Y_2, offers more goods for the same total resources A_T and B_T. For example, if one keeps X_2 constant, but moves to point Q, one increases good Y from Y_2 to Y_3. Thus, point Q represents a better allocation than does point P.

Point Q is the location of the tangent between the two production curves X_2 and Y_3. Relative to such a tangent point, it is impossible, by moving to another point, to increase either X or Y without simultaneously decreasing the amount of the other good. The locus of such tangent points, shown by the line $\overline{O_X O_Y}$, is called the "optimum allocation possibility function." Any optimal allocation, between goods X and Y, must lie on this locus curve because all points off the curve represent reductions in one good without corresponding increases in the other. The optimal relation, between goods X and Y, can be abstracted and redrawn, as shown schematically in Fig. 8-3. We shall call the Fig. 8-3 curve the "optimal-

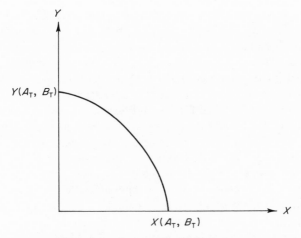

FIG. 8-3 Optimal-Choice Function

choice function." At its ends, this curve shows the amounts of X and Y obtained by allocating all resources to just one of the goods.

It remains to find the optimum point on the optimal-choice curve. To this end, one must develop a preference ranking among the possible combinations of goods X and Y. Obviously, if there is no preference, any point along the curve is as good as any other. It will be assumed that preferences do exist, and that the consumer prefers more of any good rather than less of it. If so, the combination of goods in quantities $(X_1 + \Delta X, Y_1)$ is pre-

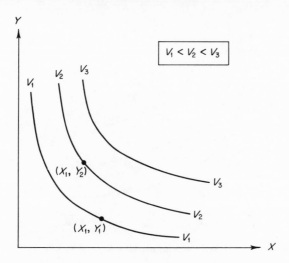

FIG. 8-4 Consumption Indifference Curves

ferred over the combination (X_1, Y_1), provided that ΔX is greater than zero. Similarly, $(X_1, Y_1 + \Delta Y)$ is preferred over (X_1, Y_1) for $\Delta Y > 0$.

Let V_1 be the qualitative "value" placed by the consumer on the combination of goods in quantities (X_1, Y_1). Since both X and Y are assumed to be valued goods, the consumer may be prepared to accept trade-offs of X and Y in such a way that other combinations of the goods have for him the same value. He is said to be "indifferent" regarding a choice among equally valued combinations. Figure 8-4 shows, schematically, a "curve of indifference" V_1 for all combinations of goods that are valued as equal to the combination (X_1, Y_1). Because of the assumption that more goods are preferred over fewer goods, the indifference curve is convex relative to the origin. Now consider some combination of goods, in quantities (X_2, Y_2), valued more highly than is (X_1, Y_1). The curve of indifference V_2, of combinations valued as equal to (X_2, Y_2), must lie above the curve V_1, again because more goods are assumed preferable over fewer. Thus, one can develop a family of indifference curves, of increasing values V_1, V_2, $V_3, \ldots$, even though one cannot ascribe a quantitative measure to these values.

If one superimposes the optimal-choice function, Fig. 8-3, on the family of consumer indifference curves, Fig. 8-4, one can obtain the optimum allocation between the two goods. This is done in Fig. 8-5. Since the con-

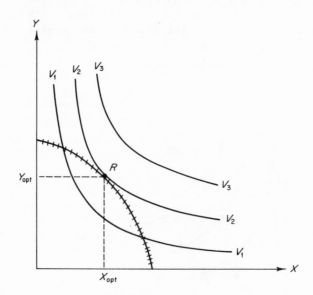

FIG. 8-5 Optimum Allocation of Goods

———: consumption indifference curve; +—+—+: optimal-choice function.

sumer seeks the greatest possible value of goods, he should choose the highest value indifference curve that is feasible. Points on the optimal-choice function are feasible. Therefore, the optimum allocation is defined by the tangent point of the indifference curve that is tangent to the optimal-choice curve. From the tangent point, R on Fig. 8-5, one finds the optimal values X_{opt} and Y_{opt} of the goods. The corresponding allocation of resources A and B is found from Fig. 8-2.

It ought to be confessed that this allocation procedure cannot be applied very readily to real situations because it is difficult to develop a calibrated family of consumption indifference curves. But if one cannot do this, one must settle for the considerably inferior approach of suboptimization under constraints, discussed at the beginning of this section.

8-3   Social Welfare Functions

An individual usually allocates and spends his resources for his own welfare. To this end, it is entirely rational for him to maximize a "personal welfare function," which aggregates costs and benefits entirely in unweighted monetary terms. The function may be profit, benefit–cost ratio, or some similar measure of utility. But government is in a somewhat different position because it holds and allocates resources on behalf of the heterogeneous population it serves. When these resources are spent, the goods obtained ought to benefit all members of that population in an equitable manner. Thus, it may be unfair for government to maximize unadorned profit or benefit–cost welfare functions.

What alternative "social welfare function" would be appropriate for governmental decisions? This question has aroused scholarly and political interest for a very long time, and there is no generally accepted answer. Here are some of the classic formulations, together with the main arguments advanced for and against their use:

1. *Simple Profit or Benefit–Cost Ratio Maximization*   The welfare function takes account of only direct, unweighted money costs and benefits. It is argued that

(a)   the approach ensures efficiency;

(b)   if income and wealth distributions ought to be of interest to the state, these can better be modified directly by tax and budget policies; and

(c)   the redistributive effects of any one project are likely to be quite small.

Opponents claim that public expenditure can be effective for income redistribution. They point out that the choice, among possible policies in supplying public transportation or in financing new housing, does seem to have a significant effect on which economic groups benefit and which ones do not.

2. *Profit Maximization with Inclusion of Secondary Social Benefits and Costs* For example, for a highway one includes environmental costs to neighbors in addition to the direct construction costs and user benefits. The viewpoint remains that benefits and costs should be weighed in money terms, regardless of who is affected. Thus, a secondary benefit of $1.00 to a millionaire is given the same weight as a $1.00 benefit to a pauper. Despite obvious political faults, this approach is often used in choosing among alternative highway projects and in planning irrigation and flood-control projects. It is argued that the method is an improvement on method 1 and that no other method is efficient, practical, and reasonably acceptable. Opponents claim greater validity for methods 3 and 4 below.

3. *Profit Maximization with Constraints* This is a fairly obvious way to incorporate a modicum of social redistribution. For example, one might select the most profitable highway route, in terms of economy in construction and value to users, subject to arbitrarily set standards for amenity to neighbors and for minority group employment in the work of construction. Both supporters and detractors of profit maximization, as a social welfare function, are troubled by this approach because the social constraints usually must be set in an arbitrary, irrational manner.

4. *Vote Maximization* The government takes a populist view and concedes that it should be directly responsive to voters. To this end, it always chooses the alternative favored by the greatest number of voters. The arguments for this approach are that

(a) it is democratic and hence "morally" good;
(b) it is especially feasible; and
(c) it tends to redistribute wealth from the haves to the have-nots.

Opponents claim that it can easily result in irrational and quite inefficient programs. Further, if the middle class outnumbers the poor, as may be the case in the United States today, any resultant wealth distribution may be such as to make poor people poorer.

5. *Democratic Strength of Preference* This is the name given by its originator Foster [6] to a welfare function, wherein benefits are to be accounted for each individual (or household) so as to reflect their value to that individual. Otherwise, all direct and indirect costs and benefits are to be weighed in purely financial terms. The argument can be shown by an example. Suppose that society's average personal income is $5000 per

person per year. Suppose further that a proposed new transit line will yield an average benefit of $5 per person per year. Consider a person with an income of $2500 who will benefit by $15. To him, $15 is twice as important as it is to the average person. Therefore, Foster suggests that his benefit should have a weight factor of two and thus is to be entered as $30 in the social welfare function. Similarly, a benefit of $5 to one making $10,000 should be entered as $2.50, and a benefit of $1000 to one making $100,000 should be entered as $50. Foster argues that this approach offers a reasonable and rational compromise between efficiency and populism.

8-4 Tracing the Benefits: The Criminal Justice System

When one seeks to improve the operation of any complex and ill-understood system, one faces the initial hurdle of not knowing at all how the system will respond to alternative courses of action. Obviously, no sensible allocation of effort is possible until the resultant benefits, or lack thereof, can be visualized. Thus, the first step in analysis is to develop a model that will exhibit overall responses to alternative stimuli.

As an illustration, consider the criminal justice system. It is a complex and expensive structure which has changed very little in the twentieth century, despite an enormous recent increase in crime and despite many improvements elsewhere in society's managerial and technical expertise. The system's resistance to change has been ascribed to its fragmentation, there being no central management to integrate its law enforcement, court, and incarceration functions. There are strong political and social reasons for this fragmentation, and so it probably will and should remain. Nevertheless, with no central management to provide guidance, the study of the total system, to see how it functions and where it might be improved, is still in its infancy.

Only very recently have there been efforts to model the total system quantitatively in the hope of improving allocation of resources and reducing the crime rate. It is reasonable to expect that the crime rate can be changed by changes in the justice system because most crimes are committed by persons who have been arrested before. We shall exhibit a pioneering model by Blumstein and Larson [2]. This model, first published in 1971 views the criminal justice system as a feedback flow process, wherein criminals and persons suspected of crime pass repeatedly through a series of stages, some of which are under direct societal control. Though the model was set up for California, the general structure would be very similar for other parts of the United States.

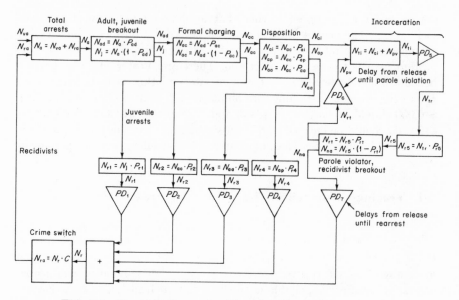

FIG. 8-6   Blumstein–Larson Model of the Criminal Justice System.

Reprinted from *Analysis of Public Systems*, edited by A. W. Drake, R. L. Keeney, and P. M. Morse, by permission of MIT Press, Cambridge, Massachusetts. Copyright © 1972 by The Massachusetts Institute of Technology.

The following presentation describes the Blumstein–Larson model as a "cohort-tracing" methodology, wherein the lifetime career of one age cohort is traced, one year at a time, from the first arrest until death. However, it also can be viewed as a population simulation model, wherein all age cohorts, each one encompassing persons born in one year, are traced together for one year's operation of the justice system. With this viewpoint, the "recidivists" (i.e., released persons who will be rearrested later), emerging from any one cohort, are viewed as rearrest inputs for the older cohorts.

The crime types included in the model were homicide, forcible rape, robbery, aggravated assault, burglary, grand larceny, and auto theft. Figure 8-6, supplemented by Table 8-2 for symbol definitions, shows the model flow structure for any one age cohort arrested in any one year. The number of persons reaching any stage, always shown by an N with an appropriate subscript, actually is a group of seven numbers, one for each of the seven crime types. Thus, the N's may be viewed as seven-dimensional vectors. This breakdown must be maintained because the branching probabilities, at several model stages, depend on the type of crime as well as on the age of the criminal.

TABLE 8-2
Key to Fig. 8-6

Variable or parameter name	Definition
N_{va}	Number of virgin arrests
N_{ra}	Number of recidivist arrests
N_a	Total number of arrests
N_{ad}, P_{ad}	Number (proportion) of arrests that are adult arrests
N_j	Number of arrests that are juvenile arrests
N_{ac}, P_{ac}	Number (proportion) of adult arrests formally charged
$N_{a\bar{c}}$	Number of adult arrests not formally charged
N_{ai}, P_{ai}	Number (proportion) of charged adults incarcerated
N_{ap}, P_{ap}	Number (proportion) of charged adults granted probation
N_{aa}, P_{aa}	Number (proportion) of charged adults released or acquitted
N_{ti}	Total number of adults who are incarcerated
N_{tr}	Number of adults released from incarceration
N_{r1}, P_{r1}	Number (proportion) of arrested juveniles who are rearrested
N_{r2}, P_{r2}	Number (proportion) of adults arrested but not formally charged who are rearrested
N_{r3}, P_{r3}	Number (proportion) of adults released or acquitted who are rearrested
N_{r4}, P_{r4}	Number (proportion) of adults granted probation who are rearrested
N_{r5}, P_{r5}	Number (proportion) of adults released from incarceration who recidivate[a]
N_{rt}, P_{rt}	Number (proportion) of adults released who violate parole and are reincarcerated
N_{pv}	Number of adult parole violators who reenter prison
N_{na}	Number of adult releases who are rearrested
N_r	Total number of those who will be rearrested
C	Rearrest crime-switch matrix
PD_1	Distribution of time until rearrest of juvenile recidivists
PD_2	Distribution of time until rearrest of adults not formally charged and who are rearrested
PD_3	Distribution of time until rearrest of adults acquitted or released and who are rearrested
PD_4	Distribution of time until rearrest of adults granted probation and who are rearrested
PD_5	Distribution of time from entrance until release from prison
PD_6	Distribution of time from prison release until parole violation for those adults who violate parole
PD_7	Distribution of time until rearrest of adults released from prison and who are rearrested

[a] Adults released from incarceration who either violate parole or are rearrested.

Operation of the model begins at year one for the study cohort, taken to be at a young enough age so that virtually all arrests are of "virgins" who have not previously been arrested. The number of such virgin arrests, in this and in subsequent years, must be estimated exogenously to the model. The model proceeds to estimate how many of those arrested are released at each major stage of the system, how likely they are to be recidivists, and—for the recidivists—the delay between release and rearrest. Finally, given the crime type occasioning the current arrest, the model predicts the crime type for the recidivist's next arrest. This is done on the basis of a "crime switch" matrix **P**, whose element P_{ij} is the conditional probability that the next arrest is for crime type j, given that the previous arrest was for crime type i, where $i, j = 1, 2, \ldots, 7$.

The calculation, programmed for a digital computer, is run recursively, one year at a time. For each successive year, the exogenously determined number of virgin arrests is added to the number of recidivist arrests predicted for that year in all the prior years' runs. The resultant total number of arrested persons is subjected to the procedure outlined in the previous paragraph. Thus, the model evolves, on a year by year basis, one age cohort's lifet`me exposure to the criminal justice system.

We now consider the flow diagram, Fig. 8-6, in somewhat more detail and indicate how some of the parameters were found. The arrest input N_a, for any one year, consists of N_{va} virgins plus N_{ra} recidivists. It should be recalled that these N's are seven-dimensional vectors, to include the seven crime types, and that the feedback arrow, for recidivists, includes *all* rearrests in the current year, as predicted in the analyses for *all* prior years. Because "juveniles" are treated differently from adults, the total number of persons arrested is split by an age-dependent probability P_{ad} that the arrest is "adult." Only "adults" reach a formal charging state, where a proportion $(1 - P_{ac})$ are released without any charge being made. Of those charged with a crime, a fraction P_{ai} is incarcerated in a state institution, a fraction P_{ap} is placed in a local jail, and a fraction $P_{aa} = (1 - P_{ai} - P_{ap})$ is dismissed or acquitted. These probabilities were estimated, for each of the seven crime types, on the basis of 1965 California data. For example, persons arrested for robbery experienced $P_{ac} = 0.59$, $P_{ai} = 0.10$, and $P_{ap} = 0.30$.

The incarceration phase was not detailed further in the Blumstein–Larson paper. Presumably, the distribution PD_5, of time served in prison, the probability P_{rt}, of parole violation and consequent reincarceration, and the distribution PD_6, of time between parole release and reincarceration for parole violation, were all estimated from California prison records.

The rearrest probabilities $(P_{r1}, P_{r2}, P_{r3}, P_{r4})$ vary with the age of the individual and with the crime for which he was last arrested. The age

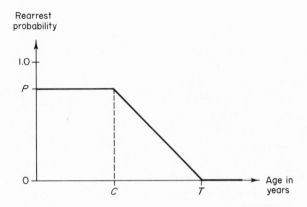

FIG. 8-7   Rearrest Probability as a Function of Age

relationship was approximated by a piecewise linear function, with parameters P, C, and T, as shown in Fig. 8-7. The 1966 Uniform Crime Reports [4] were used to estimate these parameters separately for each of the seven crime types at each of the four branch points where persons may leave the system if they are not incarcerated. For example, it was found that $P = 0.80$, $C = 35$ years, and $T = 80$ years for persons who are formally charged with robbery and who are not found guilty. On the other hand, $P = 0.57$, $C = 30$, and $T = 80$ for persons who are charged with robbery, found guilty, and placed on probation or in a local jail. Note the somewhat strange result that those found guilty have a lower probability of recidivism.

Little information was available to the authors regarding the delay distributions (PD_1, PD_2, PD_3, PD_4) for the time between dismissal and rearrest. Hence these were made fairly arbitrary constructs with a mean time of about two years, consistent with the Uniform Crime Reports for 1966.

The rearrest crime-switch matrix presented the authors with grave calibration problems because most available data were incomplete or biased. The calibration finally was accomplished approximately by using relatively unbiased data on about 500 recidivists to develop just one crime-switch matrix for all recidivists, independent of their age or previous arrest records.

Even though this model is a great simplification of reality, and the authors urge caution in the use of their numerical results, the methodology presents excellent opportunities for testing the sensitivity of crime rates and crime careers to incremental changes at various points of the total criminal justice system. For example, suppose that a test rehabilitation program has an observed effect on the recidivism rate. The model can be used to judge the extent by which crime career arrests and the imputed crime rate could be reduced if the test program were implemented on a broad permanent basis. For one such program, the authors deduce that a reduction in recidivism, from 0.61 to 0.38 of the population, will reduce total criminal career arrests by a factor of two.

Blumstein and Larson developed the model in much greater detail, complete with cost estimates for the various stages, for a simplified "linear" version, wherein arrested persons are traced through the system only once so that the complication of feedback can be ignored. The linear model still contains enough structure to enable one to study the effects, on system costs, of a wide variety of stimuli. For example, the authors found that the overall expected cost of the system is increased by $4800 for each additional person charged with robbery, that one additional rape arrest would result in an expected 0.16 additional adult-year served in jail, and that a 10% increase, in the proportion of burglary defendants found guilty in jury trials, would cause only a 0.7% increase in the number of burglary defendants placed on probation.

8-5 Designing Measures of Effectiveness: Public Health

Even where the behavior of a system is fairly well understood, benefit–cost analysis may be difficult because the various benefits are not, at first sight, at all commensurate. A good example is found in public health, where the benefits take the forms of decreased disability and longer expected life spans. The basic problem is to estimate societal costs caused by any disease under alternative postulated conditions. We exhibit here a framework for aggregating such costs, adapted from a much more comprehensive analysis by Packer [9].

Consider first one individual who is subjected to a particular disease, labeled k, under any one proposed disease-control program. He may, as a result of exposure, spend time in one or more states of disability, each of which represents to him a different cost per unit of time. A stratification of such disabilities might be into $m = 6$ states:

1. minor disability—no restrictions on normal activities;
2. restricted activity;
3. limited activity;
4. limited mobility;
5. confined—therefore immobile;
6. death.

Past data and expert opinions are to be used in estimating the expected time $E(t_{ki})$ that the individual will spend in disability state i, where $i = 1, 2, \ldots, m$, given that he was subjected to disease k. The expected time spent in disability state m, death, is

$$E(t_{km}) = \text{(expected life span in the absence of disease } k\text{)}$$
$$- \text{(expected life span, given disease } k\text{)}.$$

Let w_k be a single measure of the costs incurred by the individual as a result of subjection to disease k. A reasonable form for w_k is

$$w_k = \sum_{i=1}^{m} c_i E(t_{ki}), \tag{8-1}$$

where the c_i's are the weight factors of the several disability states.

Obviously, a crucial problem is to set relative values for these c_i's. One might seek to do this on a narrow economic basis, wherein c_i, for $i \neq m$, is the actual cost, for medical services and lost earnings, of a unit of time spent in state i. To be consistent, c_m would then have to be the expected loss due to a unit reduction in the life span of one person. But this is a very troublesome measure. If one makes it equal to expected income, there would be no penalties for the deaths of dependent, retired, or otherwise unemployed persons. Further, society seems unwilling to set a purely economic value on life. Thus, it seems impossible to avoid some degree of controversial subjective judgment in this area.

Supposing that one has somehow overcome the hurdle of scaling the components of the individual's expected cost, it remains to aggregate such costs for the society as a whole. If there are a total of N persons and if $P(n_k)$ is the probability that n_k will be subjected to disease k, then

$$E(n_k) = \sum_{n=0}^{N} n P(n_k)$$

is the expected number who will be subject to the disease. Hence one might define the expected societal cost W_k for disease k to be

$$W_k = E(n_k) w_k. \tag{8-2}$$

However, if many people are sick at the same time, there is a significant reduction in the number of healthy persons left to carry the burden of caring for them. Thus, there may be reason to replace the linear relation (8-2) by

$$W_k = \left[\frac{N}{N - E(n_k)} \right] E(n_k) w_k \tag{8-3}$$

or by some other similarly nonlinear form. This consideration is likely to be important in the future as more and more diseases succumb to enormously expensive life support programs, such as the presently available kidney dialysis procedure.

So far, perhaps the most notable effort to apply this sort of analysis to actual problems is in the United States Department of Health, Education, and Welfare. Since 1966, it has maintained a small group of economists to engage in cost-effectiveness studies for better allocation of funds to disease-control programs. As reported by Grosse [7], two measures have been used to compare alternative programs:

(1) *Program Cost per Death Averted* This was defined as the five-year program cost divided by the number of deaths averted by the program. The costs found ranged from $87 per averted death, for a seat belt use program, to over $40,000 per averted death for programs such as face and neck cancer control, increasing driver skills, and emergency medical services. The cost per death averted approach is equivalent to setting all c_i's, except c_m = cost of death, equal to zero in the formalism represented by Eq. (8-1).

(2) *Benefit–Cost Ratio* The amount saved is divided by the program cost. The societal cost of a disease is assumed to increase linearly with the number of persons affected, as in Eq. (8-2). The amount saved is the cost difference between five-year periods, without and with the program. The disability cost coefficients were made to reflect only actual medical costs and loss of earnings. Thus, the cost of a future year of "death" was set equal to the present discounted value of presumed earnings during that year.

The simple death reduction criterion (1) emphasizes the value of programs against deadly diseases such as cancer. In contrast, under criterion (2), programs against arthritis or syphilis were found to offer better benefit–cost ratios than any of the cancer programs.

8-6 Allocation of a Scarce Resource: Space for Automobiles

As discussed in Section 8-3, government is confounded by the conflicts between populism and efficiency whenever it seeks to allocate goods under its control. The problem is especially severe when the goods are very scarce and the demand is near universal. As an illustration, consider the management of limited street space. The demand by motorists for such space, on central business district streets and on some arterials elsewhere, far exceeds the supply of such space. In many cases, it is quite impossible to expand the space significantly, and thus the imbalance is likely to remain indefinitely. There are at least three ways in which to allocate this scarce resource:

1. *By Congestion Pricing* Motorists are allowed freely to use the facilities in any way they desire. The sole price paid by the individual motorist is the time that he must invest to move in a crowded environment. Where the demand for space exceeds the supply, an equilibrium is reached when traffic becomes so slow that additional motorists are deterred by the magnitude of the time they must invest in order to participate.

2. *By Rationing* Selected motorists are granted licenses to use the facilities. Others are deterred by the lack of such licenses.

3. *By Money Pricing* The user pays a charge, proportional to the distance or time of his use. The charge is made high enough so a suitable fraction of potential users is deterred by the magnitude of the fee to be paid.

At present, congestion pricing is the normally used space allocation mechanism. In some places, there is limited use of the rationing approach, whereby only some buses, commercial vehicles, and special users are permitted on certain streets during specified periods of maximum congestion. Though money pricing does exert some influence, through charges made for parking and for some "toll" facilities, there is no major example today of a congested area systematically allocating its space by this method. Yet, as pointed out by Roth [10], there is reason to believe that money pricing represents by far the best allocation procedure.

To appreciate Roth's thesis, consider any road subject to congestion pricing. It is observed, for automobile traffic generally, that the vehicles' average speed decreases, nonlinearly and quite drastically, as the volume of traffic is increased. As a result, each additional vehicle can be viewed as slowing down all the other vehicles. An appropriate measure, for this effect of congestion, is the sum of time losses for all vehicles caused by the addition of one mile traveled by one additional vehicle. Roth reports some data for central London: For light traffic, maintaining an average speed of 20 miles per hour, one additional vehicle-mile causes time losses which add up to about 1.5 minutes. In heavier traffic the losses are greater, rising to 12 minutes, at 10 miles per hour, and to 17 minutes, at 8 miles per hour, for each additional vehicle-mile.

Specifically, suppose that there is a congested central business district where the average speed is 10 miles per hour. This district certainly is not an ideal arena for pleasure driving, and so one can assume that most of the vehicles have economically meaningful tasks to perform. Thus, it would not be unreasonable to postulate about $5 per hour as the average cost of operating these vehicles. If one additional vehicle joins the traffic, its presence slows the others. Each mile traveled by the newcomer costs the other travelers a total of about 12 minutes, or $1 at the assumed time valuation. Thus, if the added vehicle itself benefits by less than $1 per mile of travel, society, as a whole, suffers a net loss as the result of its travel.

Under what conditions is the society's overall benefit at a maximum? If the traffic density were small, and the average speed great, an additional user would delay the others only slightly, and so the benefit of his trip, to himself, would probably be greater than the delay loss to others. At the other extreme, if traffic were very dense and slow, the expected gain would almost certainly be less than the loss to others. Thus, the optimum traffic volume is that at which the expected gain, to one additional vehicle, is equal to the expected loss imposed by that vehicle to the rest of the traffic.

How can this optimum traffic volume be obtained? Vehicles can be subject to a mileage tax, appropriate to location and time of day, adjusted to discourage enough of them so the remainder do travel at the optimum average speed. While complicated equipment might be required to collect such a tax with great precision, it would be quite simple to institute daily licenses—or "tolls"—to achieve an approximate optimum. By this money-pricing scheme, the limited road space would be allocated to those users who, perceiving the greatest benefits therefrom, are prepared to pay the most. The tax money collected would replace present road user taxes. These latter, being mostly charged on fuel, are not at all location dependent.

The above argument suggests that money pricing is of greater societal benefit than is congestion pricing. But, one may argue, why not rely on rationing or—if absolutely necessary—indirect money pricing by manipulation of the supply of parking spaces? The argument against rationing, to favor "essential" users, is that it is exceedingly difficult to anticipate fairly the relative merits of, say, a doctor "on call" while attending a theater, versus the operator of a rental car business. The argument against indirect pricing, via the parking supply, is that a very high proportion of central business district travelers never use the parking facilities. As Roth says, "If we wish to discourage the consumption of whiskey, we should impose a tax on whiskey. A tax on whiskey glasses might deter the fastidious, but the rest of us would be driven straight to the bottle [10]."

8-7 Conclusion

One question not covered in this chapter is how to delineate best the physical area to be treated as one entity in the allocation of resources. This question is quite an interesting one, even though rigid municipal boundaries usually preclude much choice in the matter. The smaller the area, the more one is concerned with "place prosperity," viewing the locality as an institution in conflict for goods with the outside world. The larger the area, the more pressure there is to plan for "people prosperity," without much regard for the claims of particular places. If it could be shown that the people prosperity criterion is the more advantageous, there would be objective reason to urge national take-overs of erstwhile municipal functions. Contrariwise, if place prosperity were shown to be better, then there would be a case for measures such as "revenue sharing" and the delegation of decisions to compact neighborhoods. Intuitively, one feels that the best choice is likely to be somewhere between these extremes. If so, there surely is cause to investigate how to bound optimally the decision area for resource planning. The problem has been studied on a regional–national–international basis by Whitman [13] and others, but the present author does not know of any work on the municipal–regional range of possibilities.

By now it should be clear that the optimal allocation of public resources is not something that can be done according to universally recognized scientific principles. The concept of "optimality" is quite a slippery one, despite valiant efforts by generations of economists. Some people argue that, under these circumstances, the planner should merely work out several alternatives, which then will be scrutinized by "decision makers." This seems a bit naive to the present author. The number of conceivable alternatives is always so large that the planner inevitably engages in prior selection and thus cannot avoid some responsibility for the ultimate decisions. This is a field where one cannot with honesty claim the status of a totally apolitical technician.

PROBLEMS

1. Enumerate as many costs and benefits as you can think of for each of the following proposals:

    (a) a central business district municipal parking garage;
    (b) a children's dental program, operated through the schools;
    (c) a rule that all municipal employees must reside within the town.

    If any of your measures are nonmonetary, suggest either (i) how they can be transformed into money terms, or (ii) why they cannot be so transformed.

2. A possible project: Apply the formal allocation methodology of Section 8-2 to the planning of a small community park. The resources would be a particular tract of land and assumed finite development and maintenance budgets. The goods to be allocated are:

    (a) sitting space and quiet for elderly people;
    (b) sheltered play space with facilities for young children and their mothers;
    (c) sports space with facilities for active children and adults.

    You must develop and justify your own alternative procedures for any facet of the problem where it is not possible to use the general scheme of analysis.

3. It is widely believed that the allocation of transportation funds to subsidized mass transit favors the poor at the expense of the automotive middle class. Suppose that you wished to convince the middle class that it also benefits substantially. What benefits to the middle class can you envision and how might one develop plausible measures of such benefits?

4. It is a common practice to supply police protection by use of officers, in patrol cars, who, when not responding to specific calls for help, are supposed to wait or cruise about in a useful manner. Suggest and sketch out roughly a police "patrol model" to aid in deciding how this uncommitted cruising time might best be allocated, given that the main objective is the deterrence of crime. What experiments, or presently available data, would be needed to calibrate the model? What are appropriate parameters?

5. It has been suggested that the allocation of future highway funds be done on the basis of how much motorists are at present prepared to pay for travel at the various competing locations. Present expenditure is deduced from the numbers of travelers and their mean congestion delay costs. Discuss the pros and cons of this suggestion.

REFERENCES

[1] Baumol, W. J., *Economic Theory and Operations Research*. Prentice-Hall, Englewood Cliffs, New Jersey, 1965.

[2] Blumstein, A., and Larson, R. C., Analysis of a total criminal justice system. In *Analysis of Public Systems* (A. W. Drake, R. L. Keeney, and P. M. Morse, eds.), pp. 317–355. MIT Press, Cambridge, Massachusetts, 1972; see also Blumstein and Larson [3].

[3] Blumstein, A., and Larson R. C., Models of a total criminal justice system. *Operations Research* **17**, 199–232 (1969).

[4] *Crime in the United States: Uniform Crime Reports*. Published annually by the Federal Bur. of Investigation, US Govt. Printing Office, Washington, D.C.

[5] Drake, A. W., Keeney, R. L., and Morse, P. M., ed., *Analysis of Public Systems*. MIT Press, Cambridge, Massachusetts, 1972.

[6] Foster, C. D., Social welfare functions in cost-benefit analysis. In *Operational Research and the Social Sciences* (J. R. Lawrence, ed.), pp. 305–318. Tavistock, London, 1966.

[7] Grosse, R. N., Analysis in health planning. In *Analysis of Public Systems* (A. W. Drake, R. L. Keeney, and P. M. Morse, eds.), pp. 401–428. MIT Press, Cambridge, Massachusetts, 1972.

[8] Henderson, J. M., and Quandt, R. E., *Microeconomic Theory*. McGraw-Hill, New York, 1958.

[9] Packer, A. H., Applying cost-effectiveness concepts to the community health system. *Operations Research* **16**, No. 2, 227–253 (1968).

[10] Roth, G. J., Road pricing as an aid to urban transport planning. In *Systems Analysis for Social Problems* (A. Blumstein, M. Kamrass, and A. B. Weiss, eds.), pp. 197–208. Washington Operations Res. Council, Washington, D.C., 1970. See also Roth [11].

[11] Roth, G. J., *Paying for the Roads*, Penguin Books, London, 1967.

[12] Weisbrod, B. A., *Economics of Public Health: Measuring the Economic Impact of Disease*. Univ. of Pennsylvania Press, Philadelphia, 1961.

[13] Whitman, M. v. N., Place prosperity and people prosperity: The delineation of optimum policy areas. In *Spatial, Regional and Population Economics* (M. Perlman, C. V. Leven, and B. Chinitz, eds.), pp. 359–393. Gordon & Breach, New York, 1972.

Chapter 9

Postscript

The field of urban analysis is subject to swings of fashion, wherein the predominant concerns of one period are viewed as relatively trivial as soon as new problems arise and capture our attention. This book reflects the present generation's preoccupation at trying to come to terms with the automobile age. The problem has been one of how to salvage past generations' now unsuitable urban investments. Because the automotive life is seen to require ever more space, the perceived need has been for greater efficiency in the allocation of land and other facilities so as to minimize congestion.

Inevitably, this particular problem will be less critical as time passes. First of all, society constantly rebuilds its environment, today to the effect that an ever-increasing proportion of the population lives and works in spread cities. In these, space is relatively ample, and there no longer is pressing need for most persons to have daily access to old-line central business districts. Second, at least in the United States, we are near to automotive saturation; so further usage will increase only as rapidly as does population. At the same time, we seem to be entering a period of near-zero population growth.

What will be the future fashionable problems? One can surmise almost endlessly about energy conservation and allocation, housing, and other capital maintenance in an age of affluence where few people can afford large amounts of others' labor, a social structure where man is far more mobile than are his institutions, or the problem of coping with an ever-increasing proportion of very old people. Nevertheless, the author is reasonably sure that most of the problems considered in this book will still exist, though some may be viewed as less pressing than they are today.

It would have been most satisfying to end this book with a thoughtful summary wherein everything would have been placed into its ordained niche within a well-tested scholarly structure. But urban modeling is too young, with too many gaps and too little solid verification for this sort of author's ego gratification. The embryonic state of the art is, of course, very exciting to research-minded people. Extraordinary opportunities are at hand for developing new tools, proving them, and finding socially significant applications.

Index